Nov 5/19

Martini

Martini

Jonathan Goodall

whitecap

CONTENTS

Chapter 1   **Introduction**   7

Chapter 2   **The Classics**   29

Chapter 3   **Cosmopolitans**   49

Chapter 4   **Fruitinis**   58

Chapter 5   **Sweetinis**   103

Chapter 6   **Alternatinis**   138

Chapter 7   **Savourytinis**   180

Chapter 8   **Winetinis**   190

Chapter 9   **Mocktinis (alcohol-free Martinis)**   201

Glossary   220

Index   222

Introduction

How do you get 500 Martini recipes into a book? I'm tempted to say, 250 at the front and 250 at the back, but that would be too flippant. For purists, you see, there is only one Martini, and that's the classic Dry Martini. It's made with gin, dry vermouth, and an olive. Isn't it? But there are just as many "purists" for whom olives are an abomination and only a lemon twist will do. Oh, and they'd splash in a dash of orange bitters too.

James Bond would not think twice about replacing the gin with vodka, while Winston Churchill, who would not give vodka the time of day, would forego the vermouth and ditch the orange bitters. The result? Very cold, very neat gin. You see the problem, and we haven't even touched on the sticky question of shaken or stirred?

Assuming only a Dry Martini is good enough, would you like that Dirty, Wet or, Naked? If your preference is for an olive, is yours a Franklin or a Buckeye? Or is a Gibson, with a white pearl onion, more to your taste? And as for the fact that, long before the Dry Martini came to prominence, people in the know were drinking them sweet, well, let's not even go there. I'm told that fashionable types have discovered Cosmopolitans these days and some have even moved on to Metropolitans, while others are returning in droves to the unadulterated Dry Martini, whatever that might be.

martini

The classic Martini, in all its incarnations, transcends mere fashion and, accordingly, it has a page all to itself toward the end of this chapter. But cocktail culture has boomed in recent years, leading to a new wave of neo-Martinis. To try to keep at least some of the people happy for some of the time I have divided the rest of this book into flavor groups rather than the usual alphabetical cop-out.

Fruitinis burst with fresh fruit like mango, lychees and passion fruit, while Sweetinis, with lashings of creamy chocolate, mint, coffee, aniseed, and nutty flavors, are for those of a sweet-toothed disposition. Alternatinis provide a few, well, alternatives made with base spirits straying beyond the confines of gin or vodka, while Savourytinis serve up chilies, Tabasco sauce, garlic, fresh basil leaves, and balsamic vinegar for the more experimentally inclined. Winetinis, topped up with Champagne or a splash of dry fino Sherry, are dedicated to those with a vinous bent. There are also appetizing alcohol-free Mocktinis for the designated drivers. I salute you.

History

In 1874, at the tail-end of the California gold rush, a prospector walked into Julio Richelieu's saloon on Ferry Street in the small town of Martinez. He dropped a tobacco sack full of gold nuggets onto the bar and asked for "something special."

Avoiding the ubiquitous whisky which fuelled most of the miners and cowpokes of the Old West, the bartender mixed him a small gin-based drink and, perhaps as an afterthought, plopped an olive in it. "What is it?" asked the prospector. "That is a Martinez Special," said the bartender. I'd like to think the prospector replied, "Keep the change."

The drink comprised two-thirds gin to one-third vermouth with a dash of orange bitters—and history had been made. In fact, there is a plaque in the town of Martinez, erected in 1992, which tells the prospector's story and stakes the town's own claim as the "Birthplace of the Martini."

Julio Richelieu eventually left Martinez to run Lotta's Fountain bar in San Francisco where the Martinez Special soon became his signature drink.

There are other versions of the Martini story, but I find this one not only the most convincing but also the most appropriate. It seems only right that the world's most decadent drink should arise from a frontier town at a moment of great wealth and optimism.

The strongest challenge to the Martinez version of events comes from the East Coast. It is claimed that an Italian immigrant called Martini di Arma di Taggia, working behind the bar at the

martini

Knickerbocker Hotel in New York City, was mixing a cocktail comprising gin, dry vermouth, and orange bitters just before the outbreak of World War I. Maybe he was, but this would have been nearly half a century after the Martinez incident.

The British army has also tried to claim the Martini as its own, arguing that it takes its name from the Martini & Henry rifle, standard issue between 1871 and 1891, because both drink and rifle pack one hell of a kick.

It is all well and good to argue about who invented the Martini and how it got its name, but for us drinkers the most important part of the story is how it spread. According to Barnaby Conrad III in his excellent book, *The Martini*, the first documented Martini-style recipe

was published in 1896 in New York in Thomas Stuart's *Fancy Drinks and How to Mix Them*. In it, Stuart gives a recipe for the Marquerite Cocktail comprising two-thirds Plymouth gin, one-third French vermouth (dry) and one dash of orange bitters, but quite how the name "Marquerite" might have transformed into the Martini is anyone's guess. Importantly, the news got out and by 1900 the Martini was an established concept both in the United States and across the Atlantic in Europe.

The Heublein Company had even launched a premixed Martini drink as early as 1894.

Ironically, it was during the dry Prohibition years (1920-1934) that Martinis—and organized crime—really took off in the United States. As mobsters and bootleggers took full advantage of the new draconian laws, Speakeasies (illegal drinking dens) boomed. Hard liquor became the black-market currency and it proved easier to

> **"One Martini is alright, two is too many, and three is not enough."**
> James Thurber, humorist

make passable moonshine gin than whisky. The bathtub became the last word in illicit distilling, and according to one bar book of the period, "The gin is aged about the length of time it takes to get from the bathroom where it is made to the front porch where the cocktail party is in progress."

Cocktail culture became firmly established during this furtive period as skillful mixing helped to render homemade spirits relatively palatable. They say that necessity is the mother of invention, and many classic cocktails such as Between the Sheets, Brandy Alexander and the Stinger were created during the time of Prohibition. But one of the easiest and most effective ways to mask the impurities of bathtub gin was to mix it, half and half, with vermouth (often sweet) and a slice of lemon; in other words, Martini-style.

Of course, during the Prohibition years, if a citizen of the United States wished to enjoy a civilized drink without fear of arrest the only option was to travel abroad, and this is what helped cocktail culture to cross the Atlantic during the 1920s and 1930s. In London, The Savoy opened its very own American Bar and in Paris les bars Americains were all the rage. Often, in England, drinkers would ask for either a Gin and French or a Gin and It, both of which are essentially Martinis by

40% Vol.

LONDON DRY GIN ENGLAND

another name. "French" simply referred to dry vermouth, and "It" was an abbreviation of Italian, where the traditional style of vermouth is sweet.

With the repeal of Prohibition in 1934 and the ready availability of properly-made, branded spirits, the floodgates were opened. Martinis became drier and drier as the proportion of gin to vermouth steadily increased, often to as much as four parts to one. Euphemistically put, the more gin a Martini contains, the drier it is.

This process of "dehydration" continued through the 1940s, reaching a peak with the post-war affluence of the 1950s when a Dry Martini really meant a large slug of gin with the merest hint of dry vermouth. If you drank Martinis it meant you had made it, so their consumption became a good deal more

conspicuous as the drink took on new, glamorous nicknames like the See-Through and the Silver Bullet.

Cocktails began to decline with the flower-power generation of the 1960s, as alternative recreational drugs caught the public's imagination. But this was also the time of the Cold War and there is nothing like a bit of espionage to keep cocktails cool. In a climate of mutual suspicion between the Soviet Union and the West, Nikita Khrushchev, premier of the Soviet Union (1958-1964), declared the dry Martini "America's lethal weapon."

Perhaps inspired by the "shaken not stirred" on-screen antics of James Bond, a private eye from San Francisco by the name of Hal Lipset created a Spy Martini. He explained to a 1965 Senate sub-committee: "The glass held a facsimile of an olive, which could hold a tiny transmitter, the pimento inside the olive, in which we embedded the microphone, and a toothpick, which could house a copper wire as an antenna. No gin was used—that could cause a short."

The Space Race was also in full swing at this time, as was a growing obsession with gadgets and gizmos. In 1961 the fully-automated Cocktailmatic was launched in the United States with the sales pitch: "It is now possible for the host and hostess to drink all they like at their party, and still turn out perfectly proportioned cocktails. Their hands need only remain steady enough to push the right button." I'm not sure if this sort of incitement to oblivion would get passed by many advertising authorities today.

It was also during the Swinging Sixties that the West, rather ironically, started to develop a taste for the national drink of Russia—vodka. The maverick James Bond, for example, would insist that his Martini was vodka-based rather than made with old-school gin.

> **"Hearts full of joy, hearts full of truth, six parts gin to one part vermouth."**
>
> Tom Lehrer

The sheer versatility of vodka has ensured that this trend has continued to this day, though there are signs that gin is making a bit of a comeback on the back of the trend for more "authentic" food and drink experiences. For Martini purists, of course, gin never went away.

In the 1970s, cocktails were caught in a pincer movement between economic slowdown and dubious taste. This was the "plastic-monkey" period when gaudy drinks with comedy names like Sex With

13

martini

An Alligator or, more appropriately, You're Fired, seemed to feel naked unless they sported sparklers, paper umbrellas and other naff paraphernalia.

In 1973 British prime minister Ted Heath introduced the Three-Day Week, and three years later president Jimmy Carter attacked the Three-Martini Lunch. The peanut tycoon argued that businessmen should not be able to put "$50 Martini lunches" on their expense accounts while blue-collar workers could not do likewise with their humble lunch boxes. The introduction of the breathalyzer, a growing health consciousness, and tougher work demands also imposed severe limitations on the liquid lunch.

There was a return to conspicuous consumption during the decadent years of the 1980s. With the rise of the yuppie came shoulder-pads the size of housebricks and mobile phones to match. Power dressing required power drinking and a new wave of cocktail bars sprang up in America's major cities as bartenders became known as "mixologists." The revival was well and truly under way.

The Cosmopolitan (citron vodka, triple sec, cranberry, and lime juice) became the must-have neo-Martini of the 1980s, maintaining the ascendancy of vodka over gin. It is thought to have originated on the gay scene in San Francisco, but it was in New York's legendary Rainbow Room on Rockefeller Plaza that Dale DeGroff made the Cosmo his signature drink in the 1990s.

London soon answered the call, and when the opulent Atlantic Bar & Grill opened its doors in 1994 a whole new generation of bars like Che, The Player

> ## "I must get out of these wet clothes and into a Dry Martini."
>
> Robert Benchley,
> actor

and LAB followed in its majestic wake. Master-mixologist Dick Bradsell, who tended the bar at the Atlantic when it opened, is dismissive of what he calls the "fast food" cocktail era of the 1980s and believes we're now enjoying the "epicurean" phase, a throwback to the glamorous cocktails of the 1920s and 1930s.

The undisputed king of these is the Dry Martini, proving that fashion is cyclical but style endures.

"I like to have a Martini, two at the very most, after three I'm under the table, after four I'm under my host."
Dorothy Parker

Equipment, tips and techniques

Here's a checklist of the equipment you'll need to mix the Martinis in this book, as well as a few troubleshooting tips.

• Shaker

Because all Martinis can be shaken, but not all can be stirred, I've gone for the shaking option throughout. There are occasions—when thick, gloopy ingredients like cream are used—when only a shaker is up to the job. A standard shaker is a three-piece affair with a built-in strainer in the top. Some barmen argue that ice melts more slowly in a glass shaker because glass is a poorer heat conductor than metal, but you shouldn't be shaking your cocktails for long enough for this to make a jot of difference. Vigorous shaking for 10 to 15 seconds is perfectly sufficient for successful mixing and cooling without

dilution from melting ice. The two-cone Boston shaker, incidentally, is half glass and half stainless steel.

• Mixing glass and long-handled bar spoon

Should you decide, for whatever reason, that stirring is more your thing, you will need a mixing glass and bar-spoon. You should stir briefly – again, for about 10 to 15

seconds—and gently to avoid dilution. But remember, stirring is not sufficient to properly integrate thick ingredients such as cream.

• Strainer

Whether your Martini is shaken or stirred, you will need to pour it through a strainer into your glass to remove any unsightly fruit pulp or undesirable splinters of ice. As mentioned above, a standard shaker has a built-in strainer in the top, but there might be times when "fine straining," sometimes called "double straining," is necessary. For this you need look no further than a good, old-fashioned tea strainer.

• Measure

Mixing Martinis is not rocket science. Feel free to adjust the measures according to your mood and taste, though I advise you maintain the proportions given. For sheer convenience and consistency I

recommend a thimble measure, sometimes called a jigger.

• Sharp knife and chopping board

For conjuring up twists of lemon, lime and orange and for all kinds of fruit surgery.

• Juice extractor

An invaluable piece of kit for trouble-free juicing.

• **Ice**

You'll be needing plenty of it, fresh from the freezer and so cold as to be sticky to the touch. Depending on the size of your party, you might even consider buying some ice in. And remember the golden rule —never use the same ice twice.

• **Cocktail sticks**

You don't need to impale any of your garnishes, but I feel a cherry or an olive on a stick adds a certain je ne sais quoi and facilitates the simple pleasure of stirring.

• **Martini glasses**

Serving a Martini in anything other than a proper Martini glass would do irreparable damage to the sense of occasion. It would be like drinking Champagne from a plastic cup. Martini glass sizes vary from about 4 fl oz up to 10 fl oz, but anything above 7 fl oz is unnecessary and ludicrously large. The classic 1930s cone-shaped Martini glass is a masterpiece of minimalist design and function. It is shaped this way to discourage greedy gulping and to encourage appreciative sipping while the precious contents remain above your warm hand and unblemished by fingerprints. It's a good idea to put your glasses in the cooler for an hour, or the freezer for about 20 minutes before cracking open the gin.

Techniques

Rimming

Some recipes call for the rim of the glass to be coated with sugar, salt, or maybe even chocolate powder. For sugar, chocolate powder or anything sweet wipe the rim of a pre-chilled glass with a slice of orange then dip the rim in a saucer of the chosen ingredient. For salt, use lemon or lime. Try to limit the rimming to the outer edge of the glass to prevent a mini-avalanche from falling into your drink.

Flaming

A great technique for show-offs. Take a one-inch wide strip of fruit peel, usually orange, and hold it peel-side down about four inches above the surface of the drink. Holding a lighter between peel and drink, gently squeeze the peel so that its zest is squirted through the flame, thus igniting and spraying onto the surface of the drink. Some say this enhances the aroma of a cocktail, but, what the heck, it looks great and adds a certain citric something.

Sugar syrup

Many cocktail recipes require a shot of sugar syrup, sometimes referred to as gomme sirop, to balance out the sharpness of lemon or lime juice. It can also add smoothness to a drink's texture. You can buy pre-made sugar syrups, but it's very easy to make your own. Just pour 1 lb of granulated sugar into a cup of hot water in a saucepan. Simmer it until the sugar dissolves then allow it to cool and pour into a bottle. Store it in the cooler.

Infusing

Flavored spirits, especially vodkas, are widely available but, again, it's very simple to make your own. Vodka is such a neutral, versatile spirit that it has a chameleon-like ability to adopt pretty much any flavoring agent you care to choose. For example, to make vanilla vodka put 3 split vanilla pods into a standard-sized bottle of vodka and leave it for two weeks. Turning the bottle from time to time can speed up the process. Similarly, for pepper vodka take 3 red or green chillies and cut them in half length-ways. Put these and two peeled cloves of garlic into the bottle and retire. You might need to empty a little of the vodka to make room for the ingredients, but I'm sure you'll find a use for it.

Top Tips

- Always handle glasses by the base or stem to avoid unsightly fingerprints.

- Never shake a fizzy drink.

- Always rinse olives to avoid having an "oil slick" on your otherwise perfect Martini.

- If you're squeezing oranges, lemons, or limes by hand, roll them on a surface under the palm of your hand before cutting into them. This helps to let loose the juice.

- Serve Martinis immediately as some will separate if left to stand.

- Drink 2 pints of water before going to bed.

Mixing "The Perfect Martini"

People might bicker over Bloody Marys or snipe over Singapore Slings, but when it comes to Martinis, marriages have ended. Indeed, there have probably been more bar-room incidents over this one drink than any other. Which is pretty stupid when you think about it. To express personal preferences is one thing, but if anyone tells you they know the "correct" way to mix a Martini they are a fool, because Martinis move with the times.

Early Martinis, from the latter stages of the 19th century, were comparatively sweet and would have comprised two parts gin, definitely not vodka, to one part sweet vermouth with a dash of orange bitters and garnished with an olive. Nowadays, Dry Martinis dominate and these comprise anything up to seven parts gin, or vodka, to perhaps half a part dry vermouth, possibly with a dash of orange bitters, and they are as likely to be garnished with a lemon twist as with an olive.

I believe that Martini machismo has played a significant role in the continuing strengthening of the drink—you know the kind of thing, "I can eat hotter chillies than you." Well, whoopee-do. Anyway, you can see that the choices and permutations for making a Martini are considerable.

The most macho Martini I know of is the one favored by Ernest Hemingway (now there's a surprise), which contains 15 parts gin to vermouth. It's called a Montgomery because, in his desert campaigns, the British field marshal would not attack the Germans unless his troops outnumbered theirs by at least 15 to one. Another contender would have to be Sir Winston Churchill, who displayed the bulldog spirit in many ways. When he mixed himself a Martini he would pour gin into a shaker then merely glance at a bottle of vermouth across the room.

The "in and out" method, also pretty macho by anyone's standards, is when you coat either the glass or the shaker with a splash of vermouth and then tip it

23

> ## "Happiness is a Dry Martini and a good woman ... or a bad woman."
> ### George Burns

away before adding the liquor.

James Bond insisted that his vodka Martinis should be "shaken, not stirred," while the author W Somerset Maugham was quite insistent that, "Martinis should be always stirred, not shaken, so that the molecules lie sensuously on top of one another." In truth, it really doesn't matter which method you use. The enemy of the Martini is dilution, which is why bartenders go through such a palaver to make it cold without having to put ice cubes in it. Whether you shake your Martini in a traditional shaker or stir it in a mixing glass with a long-handled bar spoon you should make sure that the vessel is two-thirds full of ice as insufficient ice will melt more quickly. You should shake vigorously or stir gently for about 10 to 15 seconds, no more. Shaking is much better for letting off steam after a tough day.

Always use fresh ice for a new round of Martinis. It should be so cold as to be sticky to the touch, and you might want to use frozen mineral water to preclude the impurities and chlorine in tap water.

The reason a Martini is then poured through a strainer into the glass is to prevent any splinters of ice getting into the drink. We wouldn't want to "bruise" our gin now, would we?

One thing we can all agree on is that a Martini should be ice-cold. To keep temperatures down you could chill your glasses for one hour in the cooler or 20 minutes in the freezer before you get shaking (or stirring). Some people suggest that you should keep the shaker in the freezer and that you shake your Martini until your hands stick to it, but I think this smacks of Martini masochism. It is also acceptable to store vodka in a freezer, but never subject gin or vermouth to this kind of treatment as their aromatics would be brutalized.

Now step with me into the garnish minefield. Firstly, all garnishes should be edible and enhance the drink. Anything else is for garnish perverts. Historian, critic, and novelist, Bernard De Voto opined, "Nothing can be done with people who put olives in Martinis, presumably because in some desolate childhood hour someone refused them a dill pickle and so they go through life lusting for the taste of brine. Something can be done with people who put pickled olives in: strangulation seems best." Me? I'm with TV host Johnny Carson on this one:

"Happiness is finding two olives in your Martini when you're hungry."

But remember to rinse your olives first so they don't give an oily appearance to the limpid clarity of your drink.

Should you prefer a lemon twist, it should have no pulp attached, as this can impart a degree of bitterness. Your twist should be a mere sliver, about one and a half inches long and a quarter of inch wide. For maximum impact you might wish to twist the peel over the surface of the Martini to release a little zest before plopping it in. It's why it's called a twist. You could also wipe the rim of the glass with a spare twist for real lemon overload.

Of course, you might prefer your Martinis garnished in the Dickensian style (with no olive or twist), in which case you could go for a Gibson, which is garnished with a white pearl onion. And remember, if you're having a sweet Martini, it should be garnished with a cherry, though god only knows what Bernard De Voto would do to you if he found out.

Here is a recipe for the timeless and classic dry Martini.

Classic Dry Martini

3 fl oz gin

Dash dry vermouth (contentious)

Dash of orange bitters (optional)

Twist of lemon peel or an olive to garnish

Method
Pour the gin, vermouth and orange
bitters into an ice-filled shaker. Shake
vigorously for no more than 20 seconds.
Your Martini should be ice-cold to the
very last drop. Strain it into a chilled
Martini glass and serve with a twist of
lemon or an olive.

Useful Martini Terminology

- **Naked Martini** made by merely rinsing the glass with vermouth then tipping it away

- **Wet Martini** made with extra vermouth

- **Dirty Martini** made with a dash of brine from an olive jar

- **Bradford Martini** shaken, not stirred

- **Gibson Martini** garnished with a white pearl onion

- **Franklin Martini** garnished with two olives, as favored by Franklin Roosevelt

- **Buckeye Martini** garnished with a black olive

- **Dickensian Martini** no olive or twist

the
classics

Absolutely Fabulous Martini

1¹/₂ fl oz gin

1¹/₂ fl oz dry vermouth

3 dashes of orange bitters (optional)

Here's a variant for those not suffering from Martini machismo, with the gin and vermouth in perfect equilibrium.

Method
Shake all ingredients with ice and strain into a chilled Martini glass. Garnish with a lemon twist.

Green Martini

2 fl oz gin

¹/₂ fl oz green Chartreuse

Here's a herbal, almost medicinal-tasting Martini based on Chartreuse from the French Alps. Made from approximately 130 plant and root extracts macerated and blended together, the secret formula dates back to at least 1605 and is known to only two monks of the Order of Chartreuse at any given time.

Method
Shake all ingredients with ice and strain into a Martini glass. Garnish with an olive (stuffed with an almond if you're feeling fancy).

Farmer's Martini

2¹/₂ fl oz gin

¹/₂ fl oz dry vermouth

¹/₂ fl oz sweet vermouth

1 dash of bitters (optional)

Method
Shake all ingredients with ice and strain into a chilled Martini glass. Garnish with a lemon twist.

Allies

1¹/₂ fl oz gin

1¹/₂ fl oz dry vermouth

1 teaspoon kummel

Featuring the freaky flavors of kummel, a liqueur flavored with caraway seed, cumin, and fennel. Caraway seed is—how shall I put this?—an acquired taste.

Method
Shake all ingredients with ice and strain into a chilled Martini glass. Garnish with a lemon twist.

Martinez

2 fl oz gin

1 fl oz sweet white vermouth

1 dash of orange bitters

Quite possibly the very first Martini-style cocktail —the one that started this whole palaver. This is the recipe proudly displayed on a plaque in the town of Martinez, California, "The birthplace of the Martini." Please note the less than macho 2 to 1 gin / vermouth ratio, and it would also have been made with a sweet style of gin called Old Tom. Legend has it, the Martinez was first mixed for a gold prospector in return for a golden nugget. I hope he told them to keep the change. According to the plaque the drink was garnished with an olive, which might put those lemon twist tyrants in their place, although somehow I doubt it.

Method
Shake all ingredients with ice and pour into a glass filled with crushed ice. Garnish with an olive.

Gin Fix Martini

2 fl oz gin

1 fl oz freshly squeezed
lemon juice

1 fl oz sugar syrup

Like the Gin Sour Martini (see page 40), the
Gin Fix Martini features the classic sweet and
sour mix of freshly squeezed lemon juice
balanced with sugar syrup. A marriage made
in heaven.

Method
Shake all ingredients with ice and strain into a
chilled Martini glass. Garnish with a lemon twist.

Astoria Martini

2 fl oz gin

1 fl oz dry vermouth

1 dash of orange bitters

Essentially, a drier version of the
Artillery Martini (see page 41).

Method
Shake all ingredients with ice and
strain into a chilled Martini glass.
Garnish with an orange twist.

White Hound

³/₄ oz gin

³/₄ oz vodka

2¹/₂ oz freshly squeezed pink grapefruit juice

¹/₄ oz sugar syrup

With the harder edges knocked off the grapefruit juice by the dash of sugar syrup, the White Hound makes a beautifully sharp palate freshener.

Method
Shake the ingredients with ice and strain into a chilled Martini glass. Garnish with a cherry.

Bone Dry Diablo Martini

1¹/₂ oz gin

1¹/₂ oz vodka

¹/₂ oz dry vermouth

1 dash of Scotch whisky

This little devil features equal measures of gin and vodka enlivened with a soupçon of Scotch. Scary.

Method
Pour a dash of Scotch into a chilled Martini glass, swirl it around then tip it out, decadently. Shake the remaining ingredients with ice and strain into the Scotch-flavored glass. Garnish with an olive.

James Bond Martini

3 oz gin

1 oz vodka

¹/₂ oz blond Lillet

Method
Shake all ingredients with ice and strain into a Martini glass. Garnish with a lemon twist or an exploding pen that fires tranquillizer darts.

Like the world's number-one spy, this Martini takes no prisoners. Also known as a Vesper, it was invented by Bond in Ian Fleming's *Casino Royale*. He named it after Vesper Lynd, a beautiful double agent, but he switched back to his vodka Martini—"shaken, not stirred"—after she committed suicide. Tragic.

Bronx

2 fl oz gin

1 fl oz dry vermouth

1 fl oz sweet vermouth

Juice from ¹/₂ orange

Said to be one of the first Martinis to use fruit juice, the refreshing Bronx is a pre-dinner favorite created in 1906 by Johnny Solon, bartender at the Waldorf-Astoria in New York. Apparently it was inspired by a trip to the newly opened Bronx Zoo. It must have been feeding time.

Method
Shake all ingredients with ice and strain into a chilled Martini glass. Garnish with a cherry on a cocktail stick.

Fifty-Fifty

1¹/₂ fl oz gin

1¹/₂ fl oz dry vermouth

Just like it sounds, a half-and-half gin and vermouth Martini for those who might want more than one drink before dinner.

Method
Shake all ingredients with ice and strain into a chilled Martini glass. Garnish with an olive.

Flying Dutchman

$2\frac{1}{2}$ fl oz genever gin

$\frac{1}{2}$ fl oz triple sec

1 dash of orange bitters

This recipe calls for genever gin which tends to be softer and fuller-bodied than traditional London dry gin.

Method
Rinse a chilled Martini glass with triple sec, then pour it away. Shake the gin and bitters with ice and strain into the glass. Garnish with an orange twist.

Maiden's Prayer

1 fl oz gin

1 fl oz Cointreau

$\frac{1}{2}$ fl oz freshly squeezed lemon juice

$\frac{1}{2}$ fl oz freshly squeezed orange juice

For unrequited lovers everywhere. "If at first you don't succeed, cry, cry again," says *The Savoy Cocktail Book*.

Method
Shake all ingredients with ice and strain into a Martini glass. Garnish with a cheerful cherry.

Dirty Martini

$2\frac{1}{2}$ fl oz gin

1 dash of dry vermouth

1 teaspoon olive juice from the jar

Here's a dry Martini for savory characters with a penchant for olives.

Method
Shake all ingredients with ice and strain into a chilled Martini glass. Garnish with an olive (what else?).

In and Out Martini

2¹/₂ fl oz gin

1 dash of dry vermouth

This is one of the driest Martinis of all, in that it has virtually no vermouth. Winston Churchill liked his Martinis so dry that he would merely glance at a bottle of vermouth while preparing them.

Method
Splash the dry vermouth into a well-chilled Martini glass, swirl it around then tip it away. You can also shake the gin with ice and strain into the glass. Alternatively, keep a bottle of gin in the cooler. Garnish with an olive or lemon twist.

Dusty Martini

2 fl oz gin

1 dash of dry vermouth

1 dash of Scotch whisky

Another Martini with a subtle hint of Scotch. Rather like the Bone Dry Diablo (see page 33), but without the vodka.

Method
Shake the gin and vermouth with ice and strain into a chilled Martini glass with a little Scotch whisky wiped around the rim. Garnish with a lemon twist.

FDR's Martini

2 fl oz gin

1 fl oz dry vermouth

1 teaspoon olive brine

Method
Wipe the rim of a chilled glass with a twist of lemon, then discard the twist. Shake the gin, vermouth, and olive brine with ice, strain into the glass and serve.

This is the gin/vermouth combination favored by Franklin D. Roosevelt, an enthusiastic imbiber of Martinis. He served Martinis to Stalin at the Teheran Conference in 1943, which the despotic psychopath described as "America's secret weapon."

Colony Club

2½ fl oz gin

½ fl oz Pernod

4 dashes of orange bitters (optional)

A sweeter Martini option for lovers of liquorice and aniseed.

Method
Shake all ingredients with ice and strain into a chilled Martini glass. Garnish with an orange twist.

White Lady

1 fl oz gin

1 fl oz Cointreau

1 fl oz freshly squeezed lemon juice

This pleasingly tart variant on the Pink Lady was created by legendary bartender Harry MacElhone at Ciro's Club in London in 1919.

Method
Shake the ingredients with ice and strain into a chilled Martini glass. Garnish with a cherry.

37

Gibson

2¹/₂ fl oz gin

¹/₂ fl oz dry vermouth

1 or 2 white pearl onions

Some believe the Gibson Martini, or "onion soup" as it is sometimes known, is named after the twin Gibson sisters who loved Martinis but hated olives. I prefer the story that it was named after artist Charles Dana Gibson who strode into The Player's Club in New York some time in the 1940s demanding "a better Martini." I can imagine the look on the bartender's face as he plopped in the onion.

Method
Shake the gin and vermouth with ice and strain into a Martini glass. Plop in a solitary white pearl onion or garnish with two on a cocktail stick, depending on which story you believe.

Fare Thee Well

2¹/₂ fl oz gin

¹/₂ fl oz dry vermouth

¹/₂ fl oz sweet vermouth

1 dash of Cointreau

A classic Martini with a tantalizing touch of warming orange. In 1951 a Martini competition in Chicago was won by a Martini served in a glass rinsed with Cointreau, served with an anchovy-stuffed olive.

Method
Shake all ingredients with ice and strain into a chilled Martini glass. Garnish with an orange twist (or an anchovy-stuffed olive, if you really must).

Paisley Martini

2 fl oz gin

$1/2$ fl oz dry vermouth

1 teaspoon Scotch whisky

A bit like the Bone Dry Diablo (see page 33) and the Dusty Martini (see page 36), only this time the Scotch stays in the glass—a positive boon for whisky lovers.

Method
Shake all ingredients with ice and strain into a Martini glass. Garnish with a lemon twist.

Rolls-Royce Martini

2 fl oz gin

1 fl oz dry vermouth

1 fl oz sweet red vermouth

$1/2$ fl oz Benedictine

An acquired taste, Benedictine takes its name from the monks of this order at the Abbey of Fecamp in Normandy. Today, the distillery is housed in a magnificent gothic palace and art museum rebuilt after a fire in 1893.

Method
Shake all ingredients with ice and strain into a chilled Martini glass. Garnish with a cherry.

Turf Martini

2 fl oz gin

1 fl oz dry vermouth

$1/2$ fl oz Pernod

$1/2$ fl oz freshly squeezed lemon juice

3 dashes of bitters

Method
Shake the ingredients with ice and strain into a chilled Martini glass. Most recipes insist that a Turf Martini should be garnished with an almond-stuffed olive. And who are we to argue?

Ginitini

$2^1/2$ fl oz gin

$1/2$ fl oz freshly squeezed onion juice

Yup, it says onion juice. Here's a drink for those who probably find themselves on their own in the kitchen at parties. Well, you wouldn't want to stand too close, would you?

Method
Shake all ingredients with ice and strain into a chilled Martini glass. Garnish with an olive.

Boston Bullet

2 fl oz gin

$^1/_2$ fl oz dry vermouth

1 almond-stuffed olive

What sets the Boston Bullet apart is its garnish; it simply has to be a green olive stuffed with an almond.

Method
Shake both ingredients with ice and strain into a chilled Martini glass. Garnish with aforementioned nut-stuffed olive.

Gin Sour Martini

2 fl oz gin

1 fl oz freshly squeezed orange juice

1 fl oz freshly squeezed lemon juice

$^1/_2$ fl oz sugar syrup

$^1/_2$ fresh egg white

Method
Shake all ingredients with ice and strain into a chilled Martini glass. Garnish with a maraschino cherry.

Gloom Raiser

2 fl oz gin

1 fl oz dry vermouth

2 dashes of grenadine

2 dashes of absinthe

Method
Shake all ingredients with ice and strain into a chilled Martini glass. Garnish with a lemon twist.

This is the polar opposite of the chirpily named Gloom Chaser cocktail (curaçao, triple sec, lemon juice, and grenadine). Instead, this is a classic Martini with a splash of absinthe, sweetened with grenadine. Absinthe—aka The Green Fairy—was the lubricant of choice among Europe's bohemian elite in the mid- to late 19th century. Such was its intoxicating influence that the cocktail hour in Paris became known as "l'heure verte," the green hour. Absinthe was favored by Oscar Wilde, Vincent Van Gogh, and Edgar Allen Poe – and it didn't seem to do them any harm …

Artillery Martini

2 fl oz gin

½ fl oz sweet vermouth

2 dashes of Angostura bitters

Possibly named after the British army's trustworthy Martini-Henry Artillery Carbine which was upgraded in 1878 to accommodate a bayonet. Sharp.

Method
Shake all ingredients with ice and strain into a chilled Martini glass. Garnish with a lemon twist.

Piccadilly Martini

2 oz gin

1 fl oz dry vermouth

¼ fl oz Pernod

¼ fl oz grenadine

Drop-dead sophistication with a twist.

Method
Shake all ingredients with ice and strain into a Martini glass. Garnish with a twist of lemon.

Gypsy Martini

2 fl oz gin

½ fl oz sugar syrup

1 fl oz chilled water

1 sprig of fresh rosemary (stalk removed)

10 raisins

Mmmmmm, rosemary and raisins—who would have thought it? But their sweet, herbal flavors are most complementary with the juniper in gin. This is a new classic, created by Jason Fendick in 2002 for Steam in London. His original recipe uses gin infused with raisins, which you could always make yourself if you don't mind waiting a couple of weeks.

Method
Crush the rosemary and raisins with a pestle in the base of a sturdy shaker. Pour in the remaining ingredients, shake with ice and strain into a chilled Martini glass. Garnish with a small sprig of rosemary.

Gilroy

1 fl oz gin

1 fl oz cherry brandy

1 dash of freshly squeezed lemon juice

1 dash of orange bitters

A sweet, cherry-flavored option.

Method
Shake all ingredients with ice and strain into a chilled Martini glass. Garnish with a cherry.

Blue Star

1¹/₂ fl oz gin

1 fl oz blue curaçao

³/₄ fl oz dry vermouth

³/₄ fl oz freshly squeezed orange juice

Stand out in the cocktail crowd with this brilliant blue number with the orange bite of blue curaçao.

Method
All together now, shake all ingredients with ice and strain into a chilled Martini glass. Garnish with an orange twist.

Jasmine Martini

1¹/₂ fl oz gin

¹/₂ fl oz triple sec

¹/₂ fl oz Campari

1 fl oz freshly squeezed lemon juice

¹/₂ fl oz sugar syrup

A colorful cocktail with a kiss of Campari.

Method
Shake all ingredients with ice and strain into a Martini glass. Garnish with an orange twist.

Kangaroo Martini

3 fl oz vodka

1 fl oz vermouth

Hard day at the office? Check out the vodka content in this one. Enough to instill new life into even the most jaded automatons.

Method
Shake all ingredients with ice and strain into a Martini glass. Garnish with a lemon twist.

Mae West Martini

2 fl oz gin

$^1/_2$ fl oz Disaronno

$^1/_4$ fl oz Midori (melon liqueur)

1$^1/_2$ fl oz cranberry juice

A voluptuous number to grace any wasp-waisted Martini glass. Mae West is credited, perhaps rather kindly, with the killer line, "I must get out of these wet clothes and into a dry Martini."

Method
Shake all ingredients with ice and strain into a Martini glass. Garnish with a lemon twist.

Pink Lady

2 fl oz gin

2 dashes of grenadine

1 egg white

¹/₂ fl oz freshly squeezed lemon juice

This frothy little number was whipped up on the opening night of a successful stage play of the same name. The Pink Lady opened at the New Amsterdam Theater in New York in 1911 and featured Henry Depp and Miss Olive Depp among the cast. Surely no relation?

Method
Shake all ingredients with ice and strain into a chilled Martini glass. Garnish with a maraschino cherry.

Naked Martini

3 fl oz gin

That's it. Gin and nothing else. Some people refer to Martinis with no vermouth as Naked Martinis. I call them neat gin.

Method
Either shake the gin with ice and strain into a Martini glass, or keep your gin bottle in the fridge and simply pour it. Garnish with an olive. Goodnight.

Oyster Martini

2¹/₂ fl oz vodka

1 dash of dry vermouth

1 smoked oyster

If you're fed up with the olive versus lemon twist debate—if it reminds you of the Lilliputians' arguments over which end to open an egg— why not toss in a smoked oyster and watch the reactions?

Method
Shake all ingredients with ice and strain into a Martini glass. Garnish with a smoked oyster on a cocktail stick.

Gimlet

2 fl oz gin

1¹/₂ fl oz Rose's lime cordial

¹/₂ fl oz chilled water (optional)

1 teaspoon ultrafine sugar (optional)

The Gimlet is a sharpener in the truest sense of the word. It's a pleasingly tart drink, possibly named after the small tool of the same name that was used to tap barrels of spirits on board British naval ships. British sailors, you will be aware, were once known as limeys because of their huge intake of limes to ward off scurvy. It all makes perfect sense when you think about it.

Method
Shake all ingredients with ice and strain into a Martini glass. Garnish with a thin wedge of lime.

Pink Gin

2 fl oz gin

3 dashes of Angostura bitters

Okay, this might not be a true Martini in the strictest sense of the word, but it looks like a Martini and tastes like one too. What more do you want? And it certainly belongs in a recipe collection for gin worshippers. Incidentally, the formula for Angostura bitters was devised by Dr Johann G B Siegert as a cure for stomach complaints. It was wholeheartedly adopted by the British navy who extended its usage beyond the purely medicinal.

Method
Splash the bitters into a chilled Martini glass, swirl, then pour out the excess. Pour in chilled gin and, hey presto! Absolutely no garnish for the pink gin purist.

Smoky Martini

2¹/₂ fl oz gin

¹/₂ fl oz Scotch whisky

No vermouth in this classic, but the Scotch more than compensates.

Method
Shake the gin and whisky with ice and strain into a chilled Martini glass. Garnish with a lemon twist.

Gin and It

1½ fl oz gin

1½ fl oz sweet red vermouth

The "It" is short for Italian, which refers to a sweeter style of vermouth, as opposed to French vermouth, which is traditionally dry.

Method
Shake all ingredients with ice and strain into a chilled Martini glass. Garnish with a lemon twist.

Anouchka

2½ fl oz vodka

⅓ fl oz crème de mure (blackberry liqueur)

A fruity alternative created by the legendary Salvatore Calabrese of the Lanesborough Hotel in London. In the great man's own words: "Named after a beautiful Russian guest who requested something strong and sweet. As I was busy at the time, I made her this drink instead …"

Method
You will notice that the vast majority of recipes in this book are shaken, not stirred, but Mr Calabrese says his recipe should be stirred. So, stir the vodka and crème de mure in a mixing glass with ice, then strain into a chilled Martini glass. Garnish with a blackberry.

Thanksgiving Martini

1 fl oz gin

1 fl oz dry vermouth

1 fl oz apricot brandy

3 drops of fresh lemon juice

Method
Shake the ingredients with ice and strain into a chilled Martini glass. Garnish with a lemon twist. Happy holidays.

Gin and Sin

1½ fl oz gin

1 fl oz freshly squeezed orange juice

1 fl oz freshly squeezed lemon juice

½ teaspoon grenadine

This citric extravaganza, using fresh orange and lemon juice sweetened with a dash of grenadine, would do a much better job of warding off scurvy than a Gimlet (see page 45). Hopefully, you don't suffer from scurvy.

Method
Shake all ingredients with ice and strain into a chilled Martini glass. Garnish with an orange or lemon twist.

Diplomat

2 fl oz dry vermouth

1 fl oz sweet vermouth

This gin and vodka-free offering may well have been created for those who need to keep a relatively clear head but do not wish to party poop. Diplomats, for example.

Method
Shake all ingredients with ice and strain into a chilled Martini glass. Garnish with a plump cherry.

Buckeye Martini

2 fl oz gin

$1/2$ fl oz dry vermouth

1 dash of orange bitters (optional)

The Buckeye's claim to fame is its off-the-wall garnish, using a black olive instead of the more traditional green.

Method
Shake all ingredients with ice and strain into a chilled Martini glass. Garnish with a black olive.

Wet Martini

$1^1/2$ fl oz gin

$1^1/2$ fl oz sweet or dry vermouth (according to taste)

Method
Shake the ingredients with ice and strain into a chilled Martini glass. Garnish with an olive or lemon twist.

No collection of classic Martini recipes would be complete without a Wet Martini. It's the opposite of a Dry Martini, meaning it contains a high proportion of vermouth. Here, I've suggested a 1 to 1 ratio but feel free to get as wet as you like. Rumour has it that this is the Martini style favored by Prince Charles.

cosmopolitans

The Cosmopolitan

1½ fl oz citron vodka

½ fl oz Cointreau

¼ fl oz freshly squeezed lime juice

1 fl oz cranberry juice

Method

Shake all ingredients with ice and strain into a chilled Martini glass.

A modern classic, the Cosmopolitan is the signature drink of Dale DeGroff, aka the King of Cocktails. He didn't invent this perfectly balanced combination of sweetness, sourness, strength, and refreshment but, during his 10-year spell behind the bar at the Rainbow Room, he undoubtedly raised it to cult status during the New York cocktail boom of the 1990s. "The recipe from the Rainbow Room menu was reprinted so often that it became the standard," says DeGroff. Others have added the odd dash of orange bitters and a splash of lime cordial, but DeGroff's version remains the template. Read it and weep.

Flamed orange twist

According to DeGroff, what set the Rainbow Room's Cosmopolitans apart from the rest was the flamed orange twist garnish. It certainly looks impressive. Cut a 1-inch-wide (2.5 cm) strip of zest and hold it peel-side down about 4 inches (10 cm) above the surface of the drink. Gently warm the zest with a lighter, then squeeze the zest by its edges. The aromatic oils ignite as they shoot through the flame and settle on your drink, the aroma of which is greatly enhanced. A little bar room magic for you.

cosmopolitans

Hawaiian Cosmo

2 fl oz citron vodka

1 fl oz pineapple liqueur

1 fl oz freshly pressed apple juice

1/2 fl oz freshly squeezed lime juice

Time to dig out that embarrassing shirt and get happy.

Method
Shake all ingredients with ice and strain into a chilled Martini glass. Garnish with an orange twist. You could replace the pineapple liqueur with fresh pineapple juice and a dash of sugar syrup while being a little more generous with the vodka. No one would be any the wiser.

Blood Orange Cosmo

1 1/2 fl oz orange vodka

1/2 fl oz triple sec

1/4 fl oz freshly squeezed lime juice

1/4 fl oz freshly squeezed blood orange juice

1 splash of cranberry juice

This punchy little number was created by Julie Reiner, a talented New York City bartender, and comes recommended by none other than Dale DeGroff, the King of Cocktails.

Method
Shake all ingredients with ice and strain into a chilled Martini glass. Garnish with a thin slice of blood orange.

Heston Cosmo

1 1/4 fl oz raspberry vodka

3/4 fl oz triple sec

1 dash of chambord (raspberry liqueur)

1 1/2 fl oz cranberry juice

1 fl oz sweet and sour mix

This raspberry take on the Cosmo comes from the Heston Bar in Indiana.

Method
Shake all ingredients with ice and strain into a chilled Martini glass. Garnish with an orange twist.

51

Kamikaze Cosmo

1¹/₂ fl oz citron vodka

1 fl oz peach schnapps

¹/₂ fl oz triple sec

¹/₂ fl oz freshly squeezed lime juice

¹/₂ fl oz cranberry juice

Just peachy. Strap yourself in; it's going to be a hell of a ride.

Method
Shake all ingredients with ice and strain into a chilled Martini glass. Garnish with a slice of peach.

Ginger Cosmo

2 fl oz ginger-infused vodka

1 fl oz triple sec

1 fl oz cranberry juice

¹/₂ fl oz freshly squeezed lime juice

For an alternative, hassle-free Ginger Cosmo substitute the ginger-infused vodka with Stone's ginger wine.

Method
Shake all ingredients with ice and strain into a chilled Martini glass. Garnish with an orange twist or a small piece of stem ginger on a cocktail stick. Go on, be a devil.

Watermelon Cosmo

1 small cup of diced, seeded watermelon

1¹/₂ fl oz citron vodka

1 fl oz melon vodka

³/₄ fl oz freshly squeezed lime juice

³/₄ fl oz cranberry juice

¹/₂ fl oz Midori (melon liqueur)

1 dash of Rose's lime cordial

4 dashes of orange bitters (optional)

Method
Mash up the melon (or muddle it, to use the technical term) in the base of a shaker, pour in the remaining ingredients and shake with ice. Strain into a chilled Martini glass, garnished with a thin slice of watermelon.

Rude Cosmo aka Mexico City

1¹/₂ fl oz tequila

1 fl oz triple sec

1 fl oz cranberry juice

¹/₂ fl oz freshly squeezed lime juice

¹/₄ fl oz shot Rose's lime cordial

This one's only a splash of cranberry and a shot of lime cordial away from being a Margarita. But I suppose that's a bit like saying a wasp is only a fluffy jumper away from being a bee.

Method
Shake all ingredients with ice and strain into a chilled Martini glass. Garnish with an orange twist.

Grande Champagne Cosmo

2 fl oz Cognac

1 fl oz Grand Marnier

¹/₂ fl oz freshly squeezed lemon juice

1 fl oz cranberry juice

No, there's no Champagne in this one, and there's no vodka either. Grande Champagne refers to the best vineyards in the Cognac region.

Method
Shake all ingredients with ice and strain into a chilled Martini glass. Garnish with an orange twist.

Cupid's Cosmo

1¹/₂ fl oz vodka

1 fl oz Grand Marnier

2 fl oz cranberry juice

¹/₂ fl oz freshly squeezed lime juice

A slightly longer, more refreshing Cosmo, enhanced by the slightly bitter orange flavors of Grand Marnier.

Method
Shake all ingredients with ice and strain into a chilled Martini glass. Garnish with an orange twist, flamed or otherwise.

Educated Cosmo

2 fl oz citron vodka

¹/₄ fl oz triple sec

¹/₄ fl oz freshly squeezed lime juice

1 fl oz cranberry juice

¹/₂ fl oz chambord (raspberry liqueur)

It's hardly going to give your gray matter much of a boost, but the judicious splash of sweet raspberry liqueur is a treat for the taste buds.

Method
Shake all ingredients with ice and strain into a chilled Martini glass. Garnish with an orange twist. To flame or not to flame, that is the question.

Limey Cosmo

1 ¹/₂ fl oz lime vodka

1 fl oz triple sec

1 ¹/₂ fl oz cranberry juice

¹/₄ fl oz freshly squeezed lime juice

¹/₂ fl oz Rose's lime cordial

If you like limes you'll love the Limey Cosmo. It's as limey as you like.

Method
Shake all ingredients with ice and strain into a chilled Martini glass. Garnish with a lime twist.

Monday Cosmo

2 fl oz vodka

1 fl oz dry vermouth

¹/₂ fl oz triple sec

1 fl oz cranberry juice

The Monday Cosmo shifts the sweet/dry balance with a decent-sized shot of dry vermouth. I *do* like Mondays.

Method
Shake all ingredients with ice and strain into a chilled Martini glass. Garnish with an orange twist.

Metropolitan

2 fl oz blackcurrant vodka

¹/₂ fl oz triple sec

1 fl oz cranberry juice

¹/₂ fl oz freshly squeezed lime juice

¹/₂ fl oz Rose's lime cordial

This blackcurranty twist on the Cosmo has the temerity to drop any reference to the Cosmo name. Could it really be that good? Like many Martinis, this hails from New York, having been created by Chuck Coggins at Marion's Continental Restaurant & Lounge.

Method
Shake all ingredients with ice and strain into a chilled Martini glass. Garnish with a flamed orange twist.

55

martini

Limon Cosmo

2 fl oz lemon rum

¹/₂ fl oz triple sec

¹/₄ fl oz freshly squeezed lime juice

1 fl oz cranberry juice

Replace the Cosmo's traditional citron vodka with lemon rum, and there you have it; a lemon extravaganza in a glass (chilled, of course).

Method
Shake all ingredients with ice and strain into a chilled Martini glass. Garnish with a lemon twist.

Plum Cosmo

2 fl oz vodka

¹/₂ fl oz triple sec

1¹/₂ fl oz freshly squeezed plum juice

1¹/₂ fl oz mixed cranberry and raspberry juice

1 dash of Angostura bitters

A veritable fruit cocktail of a Cosmo, utilizing the far-from-humdrum plum.

Method
Shake all ingredients with ice and strain into a chilled Martini glass. Garnish with a fresh raspberry.

Grand Cosmo

1¹/₂ fl oz citron vodka

³/₄ fl oz Grand Marnier

1 fl oz cranberry juice

¹/₂ fl oz freshly squeezed lemon juice

¹/₂ fl oz freshly squeezed lime juice

¹/₂ fl oz sugar syrup

¹/₄ fl oz Rose's lime cordial

2 dashes of orange bitters

It's hard to improve on the Rainbow Room's relatively simple template for a Cosmopolitan, but here's an attempt to improve on the original with the addition of bells and whistles (Grand Marnier and Rose's lime cordial) and a dash of sugar.

Method
Shake all ingredients with ice and strain into a chilled Martini glass. Garnish with an orange twist.

Sparkly Cosmo

1½ fl oz citron vodka

½ fl oz triple sec

1 fl oz cranberry juice

1 dash of freshly squeezed lime juice

Top up with Champagne or prosecco

A Cosmo with fizz does the bizz.

Method
Shake all ingredients, except the Champagne, with ice and strain into a chilled Champagne flute. Top up with fizz and garnish with an orange twist.

White Cosmo

2 fl oz citron vodka

1 fl oz triple sec

1¼ fl oz white cranberry juice

¼ fl oz freshly squeezed lime juice

Also known as a Cosmo Blanco, this is not so much a white Cosmo as a blushing Cosmo. Ocean Spray white cranberry juice is made from younger berries, harvested before they ripen to full redness. The resulting juice is less tart and a tad less assertive than regular cranberry juice.

Method
Shake all ingredients with ice and strain into a chilled Martini glass. Garnish with an orange twist.

Barney's Blue Cosmo

1½ fl oz vodka

½ fl oz blue curacao

1 fl oz cranberry juice

½ fl oz freshly squeezed lime juice

Barney's Cosmo get its citrus kicks from blue curacao rather than the more commonly used citrus-infused vodka and triple sec.

Method
Shake all ingredients with ice and strain into a chilled Martini glass. Garnish with a flamed orange zest, or a lemon twist if you value your eyebrows.

fruitinis

Alabama Slammer

1 fl oz vodka

1 fl oz Southern Comfort

2 fl oz freshly squeezed orange juice

$^1/_4$ fl oz grenadine

The late Janis Joplin's favorite tipple, Southern Comfort, is a blend of bourbon, orange, and peach liqueur. It was created by M W Heron in 1874 in his bar near La Rue Bourbon in New Orleans. The iconic label features a lithograph by Currier and Ives depicting the Woodland Plantation, built in 1834 on the banks of the Mississippi.

Method
Shake all ingredients with ice and strain into a chilled Martini glass. Garnish with a lemon wheel.

Wibble

1 fl oz gin

1 fl oz sloe gin

1 fl oz freshly pressed grapefruit juice

$^1/_2$ teaspoon freshly squeezed lemon juice

$^1/_2$ teaspoon sugar syrup

$^1/_2$ teaspoon crème de mure (blackberry liqueur)

"It may make you wobble, but it won't make you fall down," says Dick Bradsell, who created the Wibble while working at The Player in London in 1999.

Method
Shake all ingredients with ice and strain into a chilled Martini glass. Garnish with a lemon twist.

Mandarin Martini

2 fl oz orange vodka

1 fl oz gin

$^1/_2$ fl oz triple sec

$^1/_2$ fl oz freshly squeezed lemon juice

$^1/_2$ fl oz sugar syrup

1 dash of freshly pressed pineapple juice

Mandarin is probably spoken by more people than any other language; over 1 billion, and counting.

Method
Shake all ingredients with ice and strain into a chilled Martini glass. Garnish with a lemon twist.

Parisian Martini

2¹/₂ fl oz gin

¹/₂ fl oz dry vermouth

¹/₄ fl oz crème de cassis
(blackcurrant liqueur)

Paris, city of romance, sophistication, and culture. No visit would be complete without trips to the fine art of the Louvre, the medieval majesty of Notre Dame, and the sheer spectacle of the Eiffel Tower. If you have the time, pop into a bar and order one of these.

Method
Shake all ingredients with ice and strain into a chilled Martini glass. Garnish with a lemon twist.

El Niño

1 fl oz vodka

1 fl oz peach schnapps

¹/₂ fl oz blue curacao

2 fl oz freshly pressed pineapple juice

2 fl oz freshly squeezed orange juice

Top up with soda water (optional)

El Niño, the periodic warming of the eastern tropical Pacific which disrupts the weather patterns of the region, takes its name from the Spanish for "The Child" (Christ), referring to its original occurrence at Christmas time.

Method
Shake all ingredients, except the soda water, with ice and strain into a chilled Martini glass. Top up with soda, if desired, and garnish with an orange twist.

Asian Pear Martini

2 fl oz sake rice wine

¹/₂ fl oz pear liqueur

¹/₂ fl oz Poire William (pear eau de vie)

1¹/₂ fl oz freshly pressed pear juice

¹/₄ fl oz freshly squeezed lemon juice

Poire William is a sweet pear liqueur named after a variety the French call Williams Bon-Chretien, otherwise known as Bartlett. It can be either a true pear brandy, distilled from pears, or a hybrid made by infusing crushed pears with a grape-based spirit.

Method
Shake all ingredients with ice and strain into a chilled Martini glass. Garnish with a slice of pear.

Atomic Orange

1 fl oz vodka

1 1/2 fl oz Midori (melon liqueur)

2 fl oz freshly squeezed orange juice

Method
Shake all ingredients with ice and strain into a chilled Martini glass. Garnish with an orange wheel.

Green Eyes

1 1/2 fl oz vodka

1/2 fl oz blue curaçao

3 fl oz freshly squeezed orange juice

A Screwdriver (vodka and orange) with a splash of blue.

Method
Shake all ingredients with ice and strain into a chilled Martini glass. Garnish with a thin slice of lime.

Naughty By Nature

2 1/2 fl oz raspberry vodka

1/2 fl oz triple sec

1/2 fl oz cranberry juice

1 dash of freshly squeezed lime juice

Method
Shake all ingredients with ice and strain into a chilled Martini glass. Garnish with a fresh blackberry.

Raspberry Martini

6 fresh raspberries

2 fl oz Plymouth gin

1 fl oz chambord (raspberry liqueur)

$^1/_2$ fl oz sugar syrup

Method
Muddle the raspberries with the gin in the base of a shaker. Pour in the chambord and sugar syrup, shake with ice and strain into a chilled Martini glass. Garnish with a floating raspberry.

Pontberry Martini

1 fl oz vodka

$1^1/_2$ teaspoons crème de mure (blackberry liqueur)

2 fl oz cranberry juice

The Pontberry Martini was created by legendary English mixologist Dick Bradsell for the opening of the Agent Provocateur lingerie boutique on Pont Street, London.

Method
Shake all ingredients with ice and strain into a chilled Martini glass. Garnish with a fresh blackberry.

Bellinitini

2 fl oz vodka

$^1/_2$ fl oz peach schnapps

$^1/_2$ fl oz white peach purée

4 drops peach bitters

Method
To make fresh white peach purée, blanch the fruit to remove skins, remove stones and blitz in a blender with a dash of fresh lemon juice. Presto. Shake all ingredients with ice and strain into a chilled Martini glass. Garnish with a wedge of peach.

The Bellini cocktail (white peach purée, topped up with prosecco Italian sparkling wine) was created in 1934 at Harry's Bar in Venice, by Giuseppe Cipriani of the Cipriani hotel family. The drink, which was a firm favorite of F Scott Fitzgerald, Ernest Hemingway, Dorothy Parker, and even James Bond when they were in town, was inspired by the glowing pink shades favored by 15th century artist Giovanni Bellini. Offer your guests a Bellinitini; it's just fun to say.

Tainted Cherrytini

1 fl oz vodka

1 fl oz cherry brandy

3 fl oz freshly squeezed orange juice

Method
Shake all ingredients with ice and strain into a chilled Martini glass. Garnish with a cherry on a cocktail stick.

Berry Blue

2 fl oz gin

1 fl oz blue curaçao

1 fl oz chambord (raspberry liqueur)

Method
Shake all ingredients with ice and strain into a chilled Martini glass. Garnish with a fresh raspberry or a lemon twist.

Florida Rum Runner

1¹/₂ fl oz white rum

1 fl oz crème de mure (blackberry liqueur)

1 fl oz crème de banane (banana liqueur)

1 fl oz freshly squeezed lime juice

1 dash of grenadine

Method
Shake all ingredients with ice and strain into a chilled Martini glass. Garnish with a lime twist.

Grape Expectations

8 fresh seedless red grapes

1¹/₂ fl oz gin

¹/₂ fl oz sloe gin

¹/₂ fl oz freshly squeezed lime juice

1 dash of sugar syrup

2 dashes of Angostura bitters

Many of the events from Charles Dickens's early life are mirrored in *Great Expectations*, which, apart from *David Copperfield*, is his most autobiographical novel. This drink is made using grapes, so it is highly appropriate that the hero in Dickens's novel is named Pip.

Method
Shake all ingredients with ice and strain into a chilled Martini glass. Garnish with a few grapes on a cocktail stick.

Black Martini

2 fl oz blackcurrant vodka

1 fl oz chambord (raspberry liqueur)

Method
Shake all ingredients with ice and strain into a chilled Martini glass. Garnish with a flamed lemon twist.

Blackberry Martini

2¹/₂ fl oz blackberry vodka

1¹/₂ fl oz crème de mure
(blackberry liqueur)

Method
Shake all ingredients with ice and strain into a
chilled Martini glass. Garnish with a fresh
blackberry.

Pomtini

1¹/₂ fl oz vodka

1 fl oz pomegranate juice

1 fl oz freshly squeezed grapefruit juice

¹/₂ fl oz freshly squeezed lime juice

¹/₂ fl oz sugar syrup

The pomegranate (*Punica granatum*) is native
to Iran and has the highest antioxidant
content of any fruit, and even more than
green tea. A daily glass can reduce the risk of
cardiovascular disease, though not when
taken with vodka.

Method
Shake all ingredients with ice and strain into a
chilled Martini glass. Garnish with a lemon twist.

Castro

1$\frac{1}{2}$ fl oz rum

$\frac{1}{2}$ fl oz Calvados

1 fl oz freshly squeezed orange juice

$\frac{3}{4}$ fl oz freshly squeezed lime juice

$\frac{3}{4}$ fl oz Rose's lime cordial

$\frac{1}{2}$ fl oz sugar syrup

Fidel Castro is the longest-serving leader in the world today, having overturned the regime of Fulgencio Batista in 1959. Cuba, meanwhile, was the first communist state in the western hemisphere.

Method
Shake all ingredients with ice and strain into a chilled Martini glass. Garnish with a wedge of lime. A cigar is optional.

Blue Train

1$\frac{1}{2}$ fl oz gin

$\frac{1}{2}$ fl oz triple sec

$\frac{1}{2}$ fl oz blue curaçao

$\frac{1}{2}$ fl oz freshly squeezed lemon juice

Method
Shake all ingredients with ice and strain into a chilled Martini glass. Garnish with an orange twist … or a small, plastic blue train.

Peach Melba Martini

1$\frac{1}{2}$ fl oz vanilla vodka

$\frac{3}{4}$ fl oz peach schnapps

$\frac{1}{2}$ fl oz chambord (raspberry liqueur)

1 fl oz double cream

1 fl oz milk

Born Helen Porter Mitchell in 1861, the Australian soprano Dame Nellie Melba's adopted name is a contraction of the name of her native city, Melbourne. Chef Auguste Escoffier named his legendary peach and ice cream dessert after Dame Nellie, not the other way round.

Method
Shake all ingredients with ice and strain into a chilled Martini glass. Garnish with a few flaked almonds.

Star Wars

2 fl oz Cognac

$1/4$ fl oz pisang ambon

$1/4$ fl oz blue curaçao

1 fl oz freshly squeezed grapefruit juice

1 dash of freshly squeezed lemon juice

$1/2$ fl oz sugar syrup

Movie trivia: when the blasters are cocked in Star Wars it is a recording of the clinking/clunking sound of a parking meter handle being turned. Presumably a long time ago in a car lot far, far away.

Method
Shake all ingredients with ice and strain into a chilled Martini glass. Garnish with a light saber.

Cherrytini

2 fl oz cherry vodka

1 fl oz cherry brandy

1 fl oz freshly squeezed lemon juice

$1/2$ fl oz sugar syrup

Method
Shake all ingredients with ice and strain into a chilled Martini glass. Garnish with a cherry on a stem.

Pompanski

2 fl oz vodka

$\frac{1}{2}$ fl oz triple sec

$1\frac{1}{2}$ fl oz freshly pressed grapefruit juice

$\frac{1}{4}$ fl oz sugar syrup

$\frac{1}{4}$ fl oz dry vermouth

Method

Shake all ingredients with ice and strain into a chilled Martini glass. Garnish with an orange twist.

Coolman Martini

2 fl oz zubrowka (bison grass vodka)

$\frac{1}{2}$ fl oz triple sec

2 fl oz freshly pressed apple juice

$\frac{1}{4}$ fl oz freshly squeezed lemon juice

Zubrowka, takes its name from the sweet, aromatic grass munched by bison in the Bialowieza forest in Poland. The grass, which is simply left to macerate in the vodka, is thought to have a bison-like aphrodisiac effect.

Method

Shake all ingredients with ice and strain into a chilled Martini glass. Garnish with a thin, floating slice of apple, the most conducive accompaniment for Zubrowka.

Lemon Martini

1½ fl oz citron vodka

¼ fl oz triple sec

1 fl oz freshly squeezed lemon juice

¼ fl oz sugar syrup

Orange bitters (to taste)

Method
Shake all ingredients with ice and strain into a chilled Martini glass. Garnish your Lemon Martini with, that's right, an orange twist.

Scarlett O'Hara

2 fl oz Southern Comfort

1 fl oz freshly squeezed lime juice

2 fl oz cranberry juice

This is a drink created by the Southern Comfort brand in 1939 to mark the release of the film *Gone with the Wind*. Tomorrow is another day.

Method
Shake all ingredients with ice and strain into a chilled Martini glass. Garnish with a lime twist.

Sonic Blaster

1 fl oz vodka

½ fl oz white rum

½ fl oz crème de banane (banana liqueur)

1 fl oz freshly pressed pineapple juice

1 fl oz cranberry juice

Method
Shake all ingredients with ice and strain into a chilled Martini glass. Garnish with an orange twist.

Dorian Gray

1 fl oz white rum

1 fl oz Grand Marnier

1½ fl oz freshly squeezed orange juice

1½ fl oz freshly opened cranberry juice

When Dorian Gray is first presented with his portrait in Oscar Wilde's novel he comments, "I know, now, that when one loses one's good looks, whatever they may be, one loses everything … Youth is the only thing worth having. When I find that I am growing old, I shall kill myself."

Method
Shake all ingredients with ice and strain into a chilled Martini glass. Garnish with an orange twist.

Pear Shaped Martini

1 fresh passion fruit

1½ fl oz Scotch whisky

1 fl oz pear liqueur

1 fl oz freshly pressed pear juice

1 fl oz freshly pressed apple juice

¼ fl oz freshly squeezed lime juice

Method
Scoop out the passion fruit into the base of a shaker. Pour in the remaining ingredients, shake with ice and strain into a chilled Martini glass. Garnish with a thin slice of pear.

Envy

½ fl oz vodka

2 fl oz Midori (melon liqueur)

1 fl oz Frangelico (hazelnut liqueur)

1 fl oz peach schnapps

¼ fl oz freshly squeezed lime juice

Medieval theologian Thomas Aquinas said, "Envy according to the aspect of its object is contrary to charity, whence the soul derives its spiritual life ... Charity rejoices in our neighbor's good, while envy grieves over it." One of the Seven Deadly Sins, envy is linked with the dog and the color green. Those guilty of envy, apparently, will be put in freezing water when they get to Hell.

Method
Shake all ingredients with ice and strain into a chilled Martini glass. Garnish with a slice of star fruit on the rim of the glass.

Berry Exciting

2 fl oz vodka

1 fl oz strawberry schnapps

1 dash of triple sec

1 dash of freshly squeezed lemon juice

Method
Shake all ingredients with ice and strain into a chilled Martini glass. Garnish with a fresh strawberry.

Ultimate Cranberry

2 fl oz cranberry vodka

1 fl oz triple sec

2 fl oz cranberry juice

Method
Shake all ingredients with ice and strain into a chilled Martini glass. Garnish with a lemon twist.

Poker Face

1¹/₂ fl oz tequila

¹/₂ fl oz triple sec

2 fl oz freshly pressed pineapple juice

Professional advice to achieve a perfect poker face is to imagine the cold, black, dead-looking eyes of a Great White Shark. Remember, the eyes are a window to the soul —or the cards you've been dealt.

Method
Shake all ingredients with ice and strain into a chilled Martini glass. Garnish with an orange twist.

Blues Martini

1¹/₂ fl oz vodka

1¹/₂ fl oz gin

1 dash of blue curaçao

Method
Shake all ingredients with ice and strain into a chilled Martini glass. Garnish with an orange wheel.

Nancy Boy

2¹/₂ fl oz vodka

¹/₂ fl oz triple sec

¹/₂ fl oz cranberry juice

1 dash of freshly squeezed lime juice

1 dash of grenadine

Method
Shake all ingredients with ice and strain into a chilled Martini glass. Garnish with an orange twist.

Fresh Fruitini
(Multi-purpose)

2 fl oz vodka

1 cup of fresh fruit (diced)

1 dash of sugar syrup

1 dash of orange bitters (optional)

Fresh fruit Martinis took off in New York in the 1980s and were all the rage in London in the 1990s. Here's a very popular template for fresh fruitinis of any kind, though pineapple and raspberry come highy recommended.

Method
Pulp the diced fruit with a pestle in the base of a shaker, pour in the vodka, sugar syrup and orange bitters. Shake with ice and strain carefully into a chilled Martini glass. Garnish with the appropriate fruit.

Fuzzy Martini

2 oz gin

$^1/_2$ fl oz Cointreau

$1^1/_2$ fl oz freshly pressed pineapple juice

$^1/_2$ ofl oz freshly squeezed lemon juice

$^1/_4$ oz sugar syrup

Method
Shake all ingredients with ice and strain into a chilled Martini glass. Garnish with a lemon twist.

Zero Martini

2 fl oz Pernod

1 fl oz freshly squeezed orange juice

1 dash of grenadine

Method
Shake all ingredients with ice and strain into a chilled Martini glass. Garnish with an orange twist.

Glamorous Martini

1 1/2 fl oz vodka

1 1/2 fl oz freshly squeezed orange juice

1 1/2 fl oz freshly squeezed grapefruit juice

1 dash of triple sec

Method
Shake all ingredients with ice and strain into a
chilled Martini glass. Garnish with an orange twist.

Berry White

2 fl oz raspberry vodka

1/2 fl oz triple sec

1/2 fl oz freshly squeezed lime juice

Worldwide record sales for Barry White (aka
The Walrus of Love) have topped 100
million. With his rumbling bass voice and
his Love Unlimited Orchestra, Barry brought
"lurve" to the ladies of the world, most of
whom wouldn't have known his middle
name was Eugene.

Method
Shake all ingredients with ice and strain into
a chilled Martini glass. Garnish with a
raspberry.

Blueberry Martini

$^1/_2$ cup of fresh blueberries

$2^1/_2$ fl oz vodka

$^1/_4$ fl oz crème de mure (blackberry liqueur)

1 dash of blue curaçao

Method
Muddle the blueberries with vodka in the base of a shaker. Splash in the crème de mure and blue curaçao, shake with ice and strain into a chilled Martini glass. Garnish with a few floating blueberries.

Girasole

2 fl oz orange vodka

$^1/_2$ fl oz triple sec

2 fl oz freshly squeezed orange juice

$^1/_2$ fl oz cynar (an Italian artichoke-based liqueur)

Careful how you say this one. 'Girasol' is Italian for Jerusalem artichoke, derived from "girasole," which means sunflower. Cynar, meanwhile, is produced from an infusion of alcohol and fresh artichoke leaves and is usually flavored with quinine. Why not serve this one with a dish of salted sunflower seeds?

Method
Shake all ingredients with ice and strain into a chilled Martini glass. Garnish with a sunny-looking orange wheel.

Urban Oasis

$1^1/_2$ fl oz mandarin vodka

1 fl oz blackcurrant vodka

$^1/_4$ fl oz chambord (raspberry liqueur)

2 fl oz freshly pressed pineapple juice

Method
Shake all ingredients with ice and strain into a chilled Martini glass. Garnish with a fresh raspberry.

Honolulu Martini

2¹/₂ fl oz gin

¹/₂ fl oz freshly squeezed orange juice

¹/₂ fl oz freshly pressed pineapple juice

¹/₂ fl oz freshly squeezed lime juice

¹/₂ fl oz sugar syrup

"Honolulu" means sheltered harbor. King Kamehameha, having conquered Oahu, moved his court from Hawaii Island to Waikiki in 1804. Five years later he relocated to what is now downtown Honolulu. The site of the court is directly beneath the Marin building at Queen and Bethel streets.

Method
Shake all ingredients with ice and strain into a chilled Martini glass. Garnish with a slice of pineapple. It is Hawaiian, after all, making pineapple compulsory.

Ink Martini

2 fl oz gin

¹/₂ fl oz peach schnapps

¹/₂ fl oz blue curaçao

2 fl oz cranberry juice

Method
Shake all ingredients with ice and strain into a chilled Martini glass. Garnish with an orange twist.

Watermelon & Basil Martini

2 fl oz gin

1 cup of diced, seeded watermelon

6 torn basil leaves

$^1/_2$ fl oz sugar syrup

Method
Muddle the watermelon, basil leaves and gin in the base of a shaker. Add the sugar syrup, shake with ice and strain into a chilled Martini glass. Garnish with a watermelon wedge or a basil leaf.

Cactus Bite

2 fl oz tequila

$^1/_2$ fl oz Drambuie

2 fl oz freshly squeezed lemon juice

1 dash of triple sec

1 dash of sugar syrup

1 dash of bitters

Contrary to popular belief, tequila is not made from cacti. It is produced from the heart, otherwise known as the pina or pineapple, of the blue agave plant, from which the juices are extracted and then distilled twice. One litre of tequila requires between 13 and 18 lb (6 and 8 kg) of agave pulp.

Method
Shake all ingredients with ice and strain into a chilled Martini glass. Garnish with an orange twist.

Jumping Jack Flash

1$^1/_2$ fl oz bourbon

1 fl oz crème de banane (banana liqueur)

$^1/_2$ fl oz Galliano

1 fl oz freshly squeezed orange juice

1 fl oz freshly pressed pineapple juice

Named after the Rolling Stones' 1968 hit, this Martini is a real treat for the tastebuds.

Method
Shake all ingredients with ice and strain into a chilled Martini glass. Garnish with an orange twist.

Bald Eagle

2 fl oz tequila

1 fl oz freshly squeezed pink grapefruit juice

$\frac{1}{2}$ fl oz cranberry juice

$\frac{1}{2}$ fl oz freshly squeezed lime juice

$\frac{1}{2}$ fl oz freshly squeezed lemon juice

The Bald Eagle was created by Salvatore Calabrese at the Lanesborough in London for a shiny-headed customer with a good sense of humor. The Bald Eagle is also, of course, the national bird of the United States of America.

Method

Shake all ingredients with ice and strain into a chilled Martini glass. You may wish to salt the rim of the glass beforehand for an ersatz Margarita effect.

Kermit

$2\frac{1}{2}$ fl oz gin

1 fl oz blue curaçao

1 fl oz pear liqueur

When he was a child Jim Henson, creator of The Muppets, used to play with his friends at Mississippi Deer Creek, catching and listening to bullfrogs. One of those childhood frog hunters was called Kermit Scott. It's kind of spooky, isn't it?

Method

Shake all ingredients with ice and strain into a chilled Martini glass. Garnish with a lemon twist.

Desperate Martini

2½ fl oz gin

½ fl oz dry vermouth

½ fl oz crème de mure (blackberry liqueur)

Method
Shake all ingredients with ice and strain into a chilled Martini glass. Garnish with a fresh blackberry.

Kryptonite

2 fl oz vodka

1 fl oz pisang ambon

¼ fl oz Cointreau

2 fl oz freshly pressed pineapple juice

Method
Shake all ingredients with ice and strain into a chilled Martini glass. Garnish with an orange twist.

Pisang ambon is a liqueur from Indonesia made from essences of herbs and the juices of tropical fruits. Its emerald green color gives this martini its name—the drink has a similar hue to the form of Kryptonite rock most dangerous to the comic book hero Superman.

Cranberry & Mint Martini

6 fresh mint leaves

2 fl oz cranberry vodka

2 fl oz cranberry juice

¼ fl oz grenadine

Method
Muddle the mint with the vodka in the base of a shaker. Pour in the cranberry juice and grenadine, shake with ice and strain into a chilled Martini glass. Garnish with a sprig of mint.

Blue Monday

1 fl oz orange vodka

½ fl oz blue curaçao

2 fl oz freshly squeezed lemon juice

1 fl oz sugar syrup

Method
Shake all ingredients with ice and strain into a chilled Martini glass. Garnish with an orange twist.

First released in 1983, the synthpop classic Blue Monday by New Order is the biggest-selling 12-inch single of all time. Lasting 7½ minutes, it is also one of the longest singles to make the charts.

Miss Martini

1 ¹/₂ fl oz vodka

¹/₂ fl oz chambord (raspberry liqueur)

¹/₂ fl oz raspberry puree

¹/₄ fl oz double cream

1 dash of sugar syrup

1 dash of orange bitters

Method
Shake all ingredients with ice and strain into a chilled Martini glass. Garnish with a fresh raspberry.

Sisco Kid

1 fl oz vodka

1 fl oz peach schnapps

¹/₂ fl oz mango juice

¹/₂ fl oz passion fruit juice

¹/₂ fl oz freshly squeezed lime juice

¹/₂ fl oz freshly squeezed orange juice

Method
Shake all ingredients with ice and strain into a chilled Martini glass. Garnish with an orange twist.

Limetini

2 ¹/₂ fl oz lime vodka

¹/₂ fl oz triple sec

¹/₂ fl oz freshly squeezed lime juice

¹/₂ fl oz sugar syrup

Method
Shake all ingredients with ice and strain into a chilled Martini glass. Garnish with a lime twist.

Sourpuss Martini

1 ¹/₂ fl oz citron vodka

¹/₂ fl oz Midori (melon liqueur)

¹/₂ fl oz sour apple liqueur

2 fl oz freshly pressed apple juice

Method
Shake all ingredients with ice and strain into a chilled Martini glass. Garnish with a physalis (cape gooseberry) on the rim of the glass.

Lychee Martini

2 fl oz vodka

$^1/_2$ fl oz lychee liqueur

2 fl oz lychee syrup from tinned fruit

The lychee is native to low elevations of the provinces of Kwangtung and Fukien in southern China. Cultivation spread through neighboring areas of southeastern Asia, reaching Hawaii in 1873, Florida in 1883 and California in 1897.

Method
Shake all ingredients with ice and strain into a chilled Martini glass. Garnish with a twist of orange, a flick of the fringe, and an insouciant smile.

Tangerinitini

$2^1/_2$ fl oz gin

1 fl oz tangerine liqueur or syrup from tinned fruit

$^1/_2$ fl oz freshly squeezed lime juice

Method
Shake all ingredients with ice and strain into a chilled Martini glass. Garnish with a tangerine segment.

Perrytini

2 fl oz Poire William eau de vie

2 fl oz freshly pressed pear juice

Top up with Champagne

Method
Shake all ingredients, except the Champagne, with ice and strain into a chilled Martini glass. Top up with Champagne and garnish with a thin slice of pear.

Mai Lai Martini

2 fl oz vodka

$1/2$ fl oz dry vermouth

$1/2$ fl oz orange curaçao

$1/2$ fl oz freshly squeezed lime juice

$1/2$ fl oz freshly pressed pineapple juice

$1/2$ fl oz orgeat syrup (almonds, sugar and rose water)

An amended, Martini-sized version of Trader Vic's classic.

Method
Shake all ingredients with ice and strain into a chilled Martini glass. Garnish with a pineapple wheel and a cherry. Really go to town.

Alamo Splash

$1^1/2$ fl oz tequila

1 fl oz freshly squeezed orange juice

$1/2$ fl oz freshly pressed pineapple juice

1 splash of lemon 'n' lime soda

General Antonio Lopez de Santa Anna lost 2,000 Mexican soldiers at the battle for the Alamo in 1836. Among the 187 American dead was one Davy Crockett whose motto was "Be always sure you are right, then go ahead."

Method
Shake all ingredients, except the soda, with ice and strain into a chilled Martini glass. Garnish with a cherry.

Summer Martini

3 fresh blackberries
3 fresh raspberries
3 fresh strawberries
2 fl oz gin
1 fl oz dry vermouth
$^1/_2$ fl oz crème de mure (blackberry liqueur)
$^1/_2$ fl oz chambord (raspberry liqueur)
$^1/_2$ fl oz fraise (strawberry liqueur)
2 dashes of orange bitters

Method
Muddle the blackberries, raspberries and strawberries in the base of a shaker with the gin and dry vermouth. Shake all ingredients with ice and strain into a chilled Martini glass. Garnish with a mélange of summer fruits.

Razzle Dazzle

$2^1/_2$ fl oz vanilla vodka
$^1/_2$ fl oz chambord (raspberry liqueur)
2 fl oz cranberry juice

Method
Shake all ingredients with ice and strain into a chilled Martini glass. Garnish with three raspberries on a cocktail stick.

Melon Martini

1 cup ripe melon (peeled and diced)
2 fl oz vodka
$^1/_2$ fl oz Midori (melon liqueur)
$^1/_2$ fl oz freshly squeezed lime juice
1 dash of sugar syrup (to taste)

Method
Muddle the melon with the vodka in the base of a shaker. Pour in the Midori, lime juice and sugar syrup. Shake all ingredients with ice, strain into a chilled Martini glass and garnish with a sprig of mint.

Teddy Bear

1¹/₂ fl oz pear liqueur

³/₄ fl oz Cognac

³/₄ fl oz apple schnapps

1 ¹/₂ fl oz freshly pressed apple juice

1 pinch of ground cinnamon

Method
Shake all ingredients with ice and strain into a chilled Martini glass. Sprinkle over the ground cinnamon. Garnish with a thin slice of pear.

Apple Strudeltini

¹/₂ fl oz cinnamon schnapps

1 fl oz apple schnapps

1 fl oz white crème de cacao

1 fl oz freshly pressed apple juice

³/₄ fl oz single cream

Method
Shake all ingredients, except the cream, with ice and strain into a chilled Martini glass. Float the cream across the surface of the drink by gently pouring it down the back of a spoon. Garnish with a dusting of cinnamon.

Magnolia Blossom Martini

2 fl oz gin

¹/₂ fl oz freshly squeezed lemon juice

¹/₂ fl oz single cream

Method
Shake all ingredients with ice and strain into a chilled Martini glass. Garnish with a lemon twist.

Satsuma Martini

1¹/₂ fl oz mandarin vodka

1 fl oz Grand Marnier

2 fl oz freshly pressed apple juice

1 dash of orange bitters

Popular in the Fifth Floor Bar at the Harvey Nichols department store in London.

Method
Shake all ingredients with ice and strain into a chilled Martini glass. Garnish with an orange twist.

Nevada Martini

2 fl oz dark rum

1 fl oz freshly squeezed grapefruit juice

$1/2$ fl oz freshly squeezed lime juice

$1/2$ fl oz sugar syrup

1 dash of Angostura bitters

"Nevada" comes from the Spanish for "snow-capped." The State of Nevada joined the Union during the American Civil War, just before the presidential election of 1864. State motto: All for our country.

Method
Shake all ingredients with ice and strain into a chilled Martini glass. Garnish with a lime twist.

French Martini

2 fl oz vodka

$1/2$ fl oz freshly pressed pineapple juice

$1/2$ fl oz chambord (raspberry liqueur)

A classic Martini that rode a wave of popularity in the late 1990s, following in the wake of the similarly fruity Cosmopolitan.

Method
Shake all ingredients with ice and strain into a chilled Martini glass. Garnish with a lemon twist.

Nutty Berrytini

2 fl oz vodka

$^1/_2$ fl oz cherry brandy

$^1/_2$ fl oz maraschino liqueur

$^1/_2$ fl oz Frangelico (hazelnut liqueur)

1 fl oz cranberry juice

$^1/_2$ fl oz freshly squeezed lime juice

Method
Shake all ingredients with ice and strain into a chilled Martini glass. Garnish with a maraschino cherry.

Baby Face Martini

2 fl oz strawberry vodka

1 fl oz dry vermouth

1 fl oz maraschino liqueur

Method
Shake all ingredients with ice and strain into a chilled Martini glass. Garnish with a fresh strawberry or a lemon twist.

Bootlegger, liquor smuggler, psychopath, and cop-killer Baby Face Nelson (aka Lester M Gillis) stood only 5 feet, 4 inches (1 meter, 63 cm) tall. He was born in Chicago in 1908 and died after a shoot-out with FBI agents just off the Northwest Highway in Barrington, Illinois, in 1934. A short life for a short man. Here's a short Martini.

Lychee & Rose Petal Martini

1½ fl oz gin

1½ fl oz rose petal vodka liqueur

1½ fl oz lychee syrup from tinned fruit

Method
Shake all ingredients with ice and strain into a chilled Martini glass. Float a rose petal on the top, you old romantic, you.

Groovy Martini

2 fl oz vodka

1 fl oz triple sec

2 fl oz cranberry juice

¼ fl oz crème de cassis (blackcurrant liqueur)

Crème de cassis originates from Dijon in France. Dating back to the 16th century, it has been used to treat snakebites, jaundice, and wretchedness. It can also be used to add a blast of blackcurrant joy to Champagne and other sparkling wines.

Method
Shake all ingredients with ice and strain into a chilled Martini glass. Garnish with an orange twist.

Citron Dragon

2 fl oz citron vodka

1½ fl oz Midori (melon liqueur)

½ fl oz freshly squeezed lemon juice

Method
First, rim a chilled Martini glass with a little sugar. Shake all ingredients with ice and strain into the glass. Garnish with a lemon twist.

Pearl Diver

1 fl oz white rum

1 fl oz triple sec

1 fl oz Midori (melon liqueur)

½ fl oz freshly squeezed lemon juice

½ fl oz sugar syrup

Method
Shake all ingredients with ice and strain into a chilled Martini glass. Garnish with a slice of pear.

Pear & Elderflower Martini

2 fl oz vodka

2 fl oz freshly pressed pear juice

$^1/_2$ fl oz elderflower cordial

Elderflower (*Sambucus nigra*) grows wild in English hedgerows. It has been used to treat respiratory problems, rheumatic disorders, and herpes. The leaves and branches of the plant, however, are poisonous.

Method

Shake all ingredients with ice and strain into a chilled Martini glass. Garnish with a thin slice of pear.

Apricot Mango Martini

Method

Muddle the mango in the base of a shaker. Pour in remaining ingredients, shake with ice, and strain into a chilled Martini glass. Garnish with a lemon twist or a thin strip of dried mango.

1 cup of fresh chopped mango

2 fl oz gin

$^1/_2$ fl oz apricot brandy liqueur

$^1/_2$ fl oz freshly squeezed lemon juice

$^1/_2$ fl oz sugar syrup

Pineapple & Cardamom Martini

4 pods of green cardamom

4 fresh pineapple wedges

2$\frac{1}{2}$ fl oz vodka

2 fl oz freshly pressed pineapple juice

$\frac{1}{4}$ fl oz sugar syrup

Pungent, aromatic cardamom seeds, or "grains of paradise," were chewed by the ancient Egyptians to clean their teeth.

Method
Crack open the cardamom pods and muddle the seeds with the pineapple wedges in the base of a shaker. Pour in the remaining ingredients, shake with ice and strain into a chilled Martini glass. Garnish with a cube of fresh pineapple.

Pineapple & Ginger Martini

2 thumb-nail sized slices of fresh ginger

1 cup of chopped fresh pineapple

2$\frac{1}{2}$ fl oz vodka

1 fl oz freshly pressed pineapple juice

Ginger (*Zingiber officinale*) is both an anti-inflammatory and an antioxidant which boosts the immune system and increases the body's energy levels. Its beneficial properties are probably negated, however, when consumed in Martini form.

Method
Muddle ginger and pineapple in the base of a shaker. Pour in the vodka and pineapple juice, shake with ice, and strain into a chilled Martini glass. Garnish with a pineapple wedge.

French Bisontini

2 fl oz zubrowka (bison grass vodka)

2 fl oz freshly pressed pineapple juice

$\frac{1}{2}$ fl oz chambord (raspberry liqueur)

Method
Shake all ingredients with ice and strain into a chilled Martini glass. Garnish with a fresh raspberry.

Japanese Slipper

1¹/₂ fl oz tequila

1¹/₂ fl oz Midori (melon liqueur)

³/₄ fl oz freshly squeezed lime juice

¹/₂ fl oz sugar syrup

Method
Rim a chilled Martini glass with sugar. Shake all ingredients with ice and strain into a chilled Martini glass.

Orange Martini

1 fl oz citron vodka

1 fl oz sweet red vermouth

1 fl oz freshly squeezed orange juice

Method
Shake all ingredients with ice and strain into a chilled Martini glass. Garnish with an orange twist.

Pompano

2 fl oz gin

1 fl oz dry vermouth

2 fl oz freshly
squeezed grapefruit juice

Method
Shake all ingredients with ice and strain into a chilled Martini glass. Garnish with an orange twist.

Key Lime Pie

2 fl oz vodka

1 fl oz Midori (melon liqueur)

1 fl oz freshly squeezed lime juice

1 fl oz single cream

1 dash of Angostura bitters

Key limes (*Citrus aurantifolia Swingle*, to give them their scientific name) are not exclusive to the Florida Keys. They are, however, much smaller than regular limes, ranging in size from a ping-pong ball to a golf ball.

Method
Shake all ingredients with ice and strain into a chilled Martini glass. Garnish with a lime twist.

Limey

2 fl oz white rum

1 fl oz lime liqueur

$^1/_2$ fl oz freshly squeezed lime juice

$^1/_2$ fl oz triple sec

Use the Spanish Crema de Lima lime liqueur if you can find any.

Method
Shake all ingredients with ice and strain into a chilled Martini glass. Garnish with a lime twist.

Purple Haze Martini

2 fl oz vodka

$^1/_2$ fl oz freshly squeezed lime juice

$^1/_4$ fl oz sugar syrup

1 dash of chambord (raspberry liqueur)

Method
Shake all ingredients, except the chambord, with ice and strain into a chilled Martini glass. Pour a dash of chambord down the side of the glass, which will settle at the bottom to create the aforementioned purple haze effect. Garnish with a lime twist.

Leninade

10 fresh mint leaves

2 fl oz citron vodka

$^3/_4$ fl oz freshly squeezed lemon juice

1 dash of sugar syrup

1 dash of grenadine

Top up with 7-Up

Vladimir Ilyich Lenin was leader of the Bolshevik party, the first premier of the Soviet Union and the creator of Leninism, which he described as an adaptation of Marxism to "the age of imperialism." We're not sure if he would have approved of the 7-Up in this drink.

Method
Pulverize the mint with the citron vodka in the base of a shaker. Pour in the lemon juice, sugar syrup, and grenadine, shake with ice and strain into a chilled Martini glass. Garnish with a fresh mint leaf.

Kurrant Affair

2 fl oz blackcurrant vodka

$^1/_2$ fl oz chambord (raspberry liqueur)

1 fl oz cranberry juice

Method
Shake all ingredients with ice and strain into a chilled Martini glass. Garnish with a fresh blackberry.

Rhubarb & Lemongrass Martini

$2^1/_2$ fl oz gin

$2^1/_2$ fl oz syrup from tinned rhubarb

4-inch stick of lemongrass

Method
Muddle the lemongrass with gin in the base of a shaker. Pour in the rhubarb syrup, shake with ice, and strain into a chilled Martini glass. Garnish with the lemongrass stick.

Ruby Martini

2 fl oz citron vodka

1 fl oz triple sec

2 fl oz freshly squeezed pink
grapefruit juice

1 dash of sugar syrup

The grapefruit juice gives this Martini a
pleasingly bitter taste.

Method
Shake all ingredients with ice and strain into a
chilled Martini glass. Garnish with a lemon twist.

Thriller

2¹/₂ fl oz Scotch whisky

1 fl oz ginger wine

1 fl oz freshly squeezed orange juice

1 dash of sugar syrup

Thriller by Prince of Pop Michael Jackson is
still the best-selling album of all time, having
sold 45 million copies.

Method
Shake all ingredients with ice and strain into a
chilled Martini glass. Garnish with an orange twist.

Northern Lights

1¹/₂ fl oz bison grass vodka

1 fl oz apple schnapps

1 fl oz freshly pressed apple juice

¹/₂ fl oz freshly squeezed lime juice

¹/₂ fl oz Pernod

¹/₂ fl oz sugar syrup

The Northern Lights occur as a result of solar
particles, flung into space by explosions and
flares on the Sun, colliding with the gases in
the Earth's atmosphere. This spectacular
phenomenon is also known as Aurora
Borealis, a term coined by Galileo meaning
"red dawn of the north."

Method
Shake all ingredients with ice and strain into a
chilled Martini glass. Garnish with star anise.

Lemon Aid

1 fl oz vodka

1 fl oz lemon liqueur

Method
Shake all ingredients with ice and strain into a chilled Martini glass. Garnish with a lemon twist.

Swedish Blue

2 fl oz vodka

$\frac{1}{2}$ fl oz peach schnapps

$\frac{1}{2}$ fl oz blue curaçao

$\frac{1}{4}$ fl oz freshly squeezed lime juice

$\frac{1}{4}$ fl oz sugar syrup

2 dashes of orange bitters

Method
Shake all ingredients with ice and strain into a chilled Martini glass. Garnish with an orange twist.

Sling Martini

2 fl oz gin

1 fl oz cherry brandy

$\frac{1}{2}$ fl oz triple sec

$\frac{1}{2}$ fl oz freshly squeezed lime juice

An abridged version of the legendary Singapore Sling, created by Ngiam Tong Boon at the Raffles Hotel in Singapore. In the hotel's museum, visitors may view the safe in which he locked away his precious recipe books, including the Sling recipe hastily scribbled on a bar chit in 1936 by a guest of the hotel who asked for it.

Method
Shake all ingredients with ice and strain into a chilled Martini glass. Garnish with a lime twist.

Kee-Wee Martini

1 1/2 fl oz gin

2 fl oz freshly pressed kiwi juice

1/4 fl oz freshly squeezed lemon juice

1/2 fl oz sugar syrup

Kiwifruit happens to be the only thing I'm allergic to. Thought I'd share that with you.

Method
Shake all ingredients with ice and strain into a chilled Martini glass. Garnish with a slice of kiwi fruit on the rim of the glass.

Bee's Knees Martini

2 fl oz gin

1 teaspoon runny honey

1 fl oz freshly squeezed lemon juice

1 fl oz freshly squeezed orange juice

Method
Stir the honey with gin in the base of a shaker until the honey dissolves. Pour in the lemon juice and orange juice, shake ingredients with ice and strain into a chilled Martini glass. Garnish with a lemon twist.

Spiced Cranberry Martini

6 dried cloves

1 fl oz dark rum

1 fl oz cranberry vodka

2 fl oz cranberry juice

1/2 fl oz sugar syrup

Method
Shake all ingredients with ice and strain into a chilled Martini glass. Garnish with a light dusting of cinnamon.

Crantini

2 fl oz cranberry vodka

1 fl oz cranberry juice

The cranberry is one of only a handful of fruits native to North America; the Concord grape and blueberry being the others. Its name is derived from "crane berry" because of the resemblance of the cranberry flower to the head and bill of a crane.

Method
Shake all ingredients with ice and strain into a chilled Martini glass. Garnish with an orange twist.

95

Chihuahua Martini

2 fl oz tequila

3 fl oz freshly squeezed grapefruit juice

4 dashes of Angostura bitters

Native to Mexico, the Chihuahua is the world's smallest breed of dog. It might also be the yappiest.

Method

Shake all ingredients with ice and strain into a chilled Martini glass. Garnish with an orange twist.

Strawberry Martini

2 fl oz gin

1 teaspoon grenadine

1 teaspoon dry vermouth

2 fresh strawberries

Method

Rub the rim of a chilled Martini glass with a cut strawberry then dip the rim in a bowl of sugar until evenly coated. Shake the gin, grenadine, and dry vermouth with ice and strain into the strawberryfied glass. Plop in the remaining strawberry by way of garnish.

Mango Madness

2 fl oz vodka

1 fl oz Midori (melon liqueur)

1 fl oz freshly squeezed mango juice

The mango (*Mangifera indica*) is native to southern Asia, especially Burma and eastern India, and it really can't handle the cold. Its flowers and fruit can be killed if the temperature drops below 40° F (4° C), even for a short period.

Method
Shake all ingredients with ice and strain into a chilled Martini glass. Garnish with a thin slice of green melon (red would clash terribly).

Rasta's Revenge

$1\frac{1}{2}$ fl oz gin

$\frac{1}{2}$ fl oz dark rum

$\frac{1}{2}$ fl oz ruby Port

$\frac{1}{2}$ fl oz freshly squeezed orange juice

$\frac{1}{2}$ fl oz freshly squeezed lime juice

$\frac{1}{2}$ fl oz sugar syrup

Ganga (marijuana) is considered the "wisdom weed" by Rastafarians who use it as part of a religious rite to get closer to their inner spiritual self, Jah (God) and Creation. This belief is based on Psalm 104:14 which says, "He causeth the grass to grow for the cattle and herb for the service of man, that he may bring forth food out of the earth."

Method
Shake all ingredients with ice and strain into a chilled Martini glass. Garnish with a lemon twist.

Tahititini

2 fl oz white rum

$\frac{1}{2}$ fl oz freshly squeezed lemon juice

$\frac{1}{2}$ fl oz freshly squeezed lime juice

$\frac{1}{2}$ fl oz freshly pressed pineapple juice

1 dash of maraschino liqueur

The mutinous ship, *The Bounty*, reached Tahiti in 1788 to collect its cargo of breadfruit. A scientist of the time said of the Tahitians that they know "no other god but love; every day is consecrated to it, the whole island is its temple, all the women are its idols, all the men its worshippers." The rest, as they say, is history.

Method
Shake all ingredients with ice and strain into a chilled Martini glass. Garnish with a lime twist or a cherry.

Berritini

2 fl oz blackcurrant vodka

1 fl oz chambord (raspberry liqueur)

$\frac{1}{2}$ fl oz freshly squeezed lemon juice

Method
Rim a chilled Martini glass with ultrafine sugar. Shake all ingredients with ice and strain into the glass. Garnish with a fresh raspberry or a lemon twist.

Peach Blossom Martini

$2\frac{1}{2}$ fl oz peach vodka

$\frac{1}{2}$ fl oz red Dubonnet

$\frac{1}{2}$ fl oz maraschino liqueur

Method
Shake all ingredients with ice and strain into a chilled Martini glass. Garnish with a thin slice of peach.

Tango Martini

$1\frac{1}{2}$ fl oz gin

1 fl oz sweet red vermouth

1 fl oz dry vermouth

$\frac{1}{2}$ fl oz orange curaçao

Juice of 1 orange

Method
Squeeze the orange juice into a chilled Martini glass. Shake the gin, orange curacao, and two shades of vermouth with ice and strain into the glass. Garnish with an orange twist.

Mitch Martini

2 fl oz zubrowka (bison grass vodka)

1 1/2 fl oz freshly pressed apple juice

1/2 fl oz passion fruit syrup

1/4 fl oz peach schnapps

1/2 fl oz freshly squeezed lemon juice

Zubrowka, the Polish word for bison grass vodka, is derived from "zubr," meaning bison. The Poles favor apple as the perfect accompaniment for Zubrowka as its tartness works especially well with the inherent sweetness of the grass. Tatanka is a traditional Polish cocktail comprising one part Zubrowka to two parts apple juice.

Method
Shake all ingredients with ice and strain into a chilled Martini glass. Garnish with an apple wedge.

Tequila Fanny Banger

1 fl oz tequila

1 fl oz vodka

1 fl oz Midori (melon liqueur)

1 dash of triple sec

1 dash of freshly squeezed lime juice

Method
Shake all ingredients with ice and strain into a chilled Martini glass. Garnish with a lime twist.

San Francisco Martini

1 fl oz sloe gin

1 fl oz sweet vermouth

1 fl oz dry vermouth

1 dash of orange bitters

Method
Shake all ingredients with ice and strain into a chilled Martini glass. Garnish with a cherry.

Top Banana Martini

2 fl oz vodka

1 fl oz crème de banane (banana liqueur)

1 fl oz cranberry juice

Method
Shake all ingredients with ice and strain into a chilled Martini glass. Garnish with a banana slice. Legend has it that you can prevent banana slices from going brown by tossing them with fresh lemon juice and keeping them in the cooler.

Florida Twist Martini

1½ fl oz orange vodka

1½ fl oz lemon vodka

Method
Shake all ingredients with ice and strain into a chilled Martini glass. Garnish with an orange or lemon twist. Or both, if you like.

Honeydew Martini

2½ fl oz vodka

½ fl oz triple sec

½ fl oz Midori (melon liqueur)

Method
Shake all ingredients with ice and strain into a chilled Martini glass. Garnish with a lemon twist.

Granny's Martini

1½ fl oz white rum

¼ fl oz cinnamon schnapps

½ fl oz apple schnapps

2 fl oz freshly pressed apple juice

Method
Shake all ingredients with ice and strain into a chilled Martini glass. Garnish with a thin slice of apple floating on the surface of the drink.

Vesuvio

1 fl oz white rum

$^1/_2$ fl oz sweet vermouth

1 fl oz freshly squeezed lemon juice

$^1/_2$ fl oz sugar syrup

1 fresh egg white

The catastrophic eruption of Vesuvius in 79CE buried the cities of Herculaneum and Pompeii and was the first volcanic eruption to be described in detail by an eye witness. Pliny the Younger recounted how the fleeing people tied pillows to their heads to protect them from showers of falling rocks.

Method
Shake all the ingredients with ice and strain into a chilled Martini glass. Garnish with a lemon twist.

Jacques Cousteau

2 fl oz vodka

1 fl oz blue curaçao

1 fl oz freshly squeezed pink grapefruit juice

With his red woolly hat and creased brown good looks, captain Jacques-Yves Cousteau brought the oceans of the world into our front rooms in the 1970s. He was one of the first major players in the environmental movement, so he deserves a big "cheers."

Method
Shake all ingredients with ice and strain into a chilled Martini glass. Garnish with a lemon twist.

Aviation

$2^1/_2$ fl oz gin

$1^1/_2$ fl oz freshly squeezed lemon juice

$^1/_2$ fl oz maraschino liqueur

$^1/_2$ fl oz sugar syrup

A retro Martini that enjoyed another 15 minutes of fashionability in London around the time of the new millennium.

Method
Shake all ingredients with ice and strain into a chilled Martini glass. Garnish with a lemon twist.

Absinthe Minded

2 fl oz vodka

1 fl oz absinthe

$^1/_2$ fl oz cranberry juice

$^1/_2$ fl oz blue curaçao

Absinthe enjoys its checkered reputation—name a country and it's been banned there at one time or another—because of its unique intoxicating properties. As well as its fearsome alcohol content it also contains thujone which has a chemical structure very similar to tetrahydrocannibinol (THC), the active compound in cannabis. Some absinthe drinkers claim to experience "clarity" and "a heightened state of mind"' while others get hallucinations and the heebie-jeebies.

Method
Shake all ingredients with ice and strain into a chilled Martini glass. Garnish with an orange twist.

Zakuski Martini

1 inch of peeled cucumber, chopped

2$^1/_2$ fl oz citron vodka

$^1/_2$ fl oz triple sec

$^1/_2$ fl oz freshly squeezed lemon juice

$^1/_4$ fl oz sugar syrup

Zakuski is Russian for "piece" or "morsel" and describes the Russian equivalent of tapas or hors d'oevres. These usually comprise cheese, anchovies, cucumber slices, and blinis topped with caviar, served, of course, with chilled vodka.

Method
Muddle the cucumber and citron vodka in the base of a shaker. Pour in the lemon juice, triple sec, and sugar syrup, shake with ice and strain into a chilled Martini glass. Garnish with a lemon twist or a strip of cucumber peel.

Fruit Salad Martini

1 fl oz vodka

2 fl oz sour apple schnapps

2 fl oz banana liqueur

Method
Shake all ingredients with ice and strain into a chilled Martini glass. Garnish with a small slice of banana. Why not?

sweetinis

Mama's Martini

3 fl oz vanilla vodka

$^1/_2$ fl oz apricot brandy

5 dashes of Angostura bitters

5 dashes of freshly squeezed lemon juice

Method
Shake all ingredients with ice and strain into a chilled Martini glass. Garnish with a lemon twist.

Trifle Martini

$2^1/_2$ oz blackcurrant vodka

2 oz Drambuie (cream liqueur)

$^1/_2$ oz chambord (raspberry liqueur)

Trifle is a quintessentially English dessert made with thick custard, fruit, sponge cake, jelly, and whipped cream. When lashings of sherry are added it is called Sherry Trifle or High Church. Trifle also means "a little"; hence, a man walks into the doctors with a dollop of whipped cream in one ear and a piece of sponge cake in the other. "You'll have to speak up," he says. "I'm a trifle deaf." Maybe you have to be English...

Method
Shake all ingredients with ice and strain into a chilled Martini glass. Garnish with a cherry.

Alexander the Great

2 fl oz vodka

1 fl oz Kahlua (coffee liqueur)

1 fl oz white crème de cacao (chocolate liqueur)

1 fl oz double cream

Method
Shake all ingredients with ice and strain into a chilled Martini glass. Garnish with a few coffee beans.

Peanut & Maple Martini

¹/₂ teaspoon smooth peanut butter

¹/₂ teaspoon runny honey

2¹/₂ oz vodka

1 oz maple syrup

¹/₂ oz crème de banane
(banana liqueur)

Method
Stir the honey and peanut butter with vodka in the base of a shaker. Pour in the maple syrup and crème de banane, shake ingredients with ice and strain into a chilled Martini glass.

International Incident

1 oz vodka

³/₄ oz Kahlua (coffee liqueur)

³/₄ oz amaretto (almond liqueur)

³/₄ oz Frangelico (hazelnut liqueur)

1¹/₂ oz Baileys Irish Cream

Method
Shake all ingredients with ice and strain into a chilled Martini glass. Garnish with a couple of coffee beans.

Zeus Martini

20 raisins

1 oz Fernet Branca
(spirit made from over 40 herbs)

2 oz Cognac

¹/₄ oz maple syrup

¹/₄ oz Kahlua (coffee liqueur)

1¹/₂ oz chilled water (optional)

Method
Rinse a chilled Martini glass with the Fernet Branca, then tip it away. Muddle the raisins with the Cognac in the base of a shaker. Pour in the maple syrup, coffee liqueur, and chilled water, shake all ingredients with ice and strain into a chilled Martini glass. Garnish with a few coffee beans.

Candy Apple Martini

1 fl oz cinnamon vodka

1 fl oz sour apple schnapps

$^1/_2$ fl oz amaretto (almond liqueur)

2 fl oz freshly pressed apple juice

Method
Shake all ingredients with ice and strain into a chilled Martini glass. Garnish with an apple slice.

Cinnamon (*Cinnamomum zeyclanicum*) is the inner bark of a tropical evergreen tree native to Sri Lanka. It grows best along the coastal strip near Colombo. In the ancient world, its rarity meant that cinnamon was more precious than gold, which explains why Nero, emperor of Rome, burnt a year's supply of the spice on his wife's funeral pyre. Spot the guilty conscience.

Banoffeetini

2 fl oz vanilla vodka

$^3/_4$ fl oz Teichenne (butterscotch schnapps)

$^3/_4$ fl oz crème de banane (banana liqueur)

1 teaspoon maple syrup

$^1/_2$ fl oz double cream

$^1/_2$ fl oz milk

Quarter of a fresh banana

Method
Mash the banana in the base of a shaker. Pour in the vanilla vodka, butterscotch schnapps, crème de banane, maple syrup, cream and milk, shake with ice and strain into a chilled Martini glass. Garnish with a dusting of chocolate powder or butterscotch chips.

Orgasmatini

2 fl oz vodka

1 fl oz white crème de cacao (chocolate liqueur)

1 fl oz Baileys Irish Cream

Method
Shake all ingredients with ice and strain into a chilled Martini glass. Garnish with a sprinkling of chocolate powder.

Hyde & Seek Martini

2 fl oz Passoa (passion fruit liqueur)

$^1/_2$ fl oz Kahlua (coffee liqueur)

1 fl oz double cream

1 fl oz milk

Method

Shake all ingredients with ice and strain into a chilled Martini glass. Garnish with an orange twist.

Coppertone Tan Martini

$1^1/_2$ fl oz golden rum

$1^1/_2$ fl oz amaretto (almond liqueur)

Australian scientists at Monash University, just outside Melbourne, have created Melanotan, a wonder drug that gives users an instant tan without having to brave the harmful effects of hours spent baking in the sun. Nicknamed the *Barbie Drug*, it triggers the production of melanin, the dark pigment, in the skin.

Method

Shake all ingredients with ice and strain into a chilled Martini glass. Garnish with an orange twist.

Blush Martini

$1^1/_2$ fl oz vodka

$^1/_2$ fl oz vanilla schnapps

$^1/_2$ fl oz amaretto

$^1/_2$ fl oz cranberry juice

$^3/_4$ fl oz milk

$^3/_4$ fl oz double cream

Blushing is caused when a release of adrenalin causes the capillaries beneath the skin to widen, causing more blood to accumulate.

Method

Shake all ingredients with ice and strain into a chilled Martini glass. Garnish with a dusting of powdered cinnamon.

Cocuba

2 fl oz golden rum

1¹/₂ fl oz Malibu

³/₄ fl oz white crème de cacao
(chocolate liqueur)

¹/₂ fl oz Frangelico (hazelnut liqueur)

Desiccated coconut for rimming the glass

Method
To rim the chilled glass, moisten the rim with
either water or a wedge of orange and then
dip it, upturned, in a saucer of desiccated
coconut. Shake the rum, Malibu, Frangelico,
and crème de cacao with ice and strain into
the glass.

Bourbon Bon Bon

2 fl oz vodka

1 fl oz bourbon

1 fl oz white crème de cacao
(chocolate liqueur)

¹/₂ fl oz dry vermouth

Method
Shake all ingredients with ice and strain into a
chilled Martini glass. Garnish with a little
shaved chocolate or a cherry.

Scotch Bounty Martini

1¹/₂ fl oz Scotch whisky

1 fl oz white crème de cacao
(chocolate liqueur)

¹/₂ fl oz Malibu

2 fl oz freshly squeezed orange juice

1 dash of grenadine

Method
Shake all ingredients with ice and strain into a
chilled Martini glass. Garnish with an orange
twist.

Walnut Martini

2½ fl oz vodka

1 fl oz Benoit Serres (walnut liqueur)

1 fl oz Tuaca (vanilla citrus liqueur)

Method
Shake all ingredients with ice and strain into a chilled Martini glass. This is such an unusual flavor that a garnish would seem superfluous.

White Stinger

2½ fl oz vodka

¾ fl oz white crème de menthe

¾ fl oz white crème de cacao (chocolate liqueur)

Method
Shake all ingredients with ice and strain into a chilled Martini glass.

Burnt Almond Martini

1½ fl oz vodka

½fl oz coffee liqueur

½ fl oz Baileys Irish Cream

½ fl oz amaretto

2 fl oz double cream

Baileys Irish Cream was launched in Dublin in 1974, single-handedly creating the concept of cream liqueurs. It is a blend of Irish whiskey and Irish cream. In its first year of production about 72,000 bottles were produced; today, over twice that number are bottled in a single day.

Method
Shake all ingredients with ice and strain into a chilled Martini glass. Garnish with grated nutmeg.

Fantasitini

2 fl oz vanilla vodka

1 fl oz white crème de cacao (chocolate liqueur)

1 fl oz Jägermeister (herbal liqueur)

Method
Pour the Jägermeister into a chilled Martini glass. Shake the vanilla vodka and white crème de cacao with ice and pour slowly over the Jägermeister for a groovy layered effect.

Black Beard Martini

2$\frac{1}{2}$ fl oz vodka

1$\frac{1}{2}$ fl oz dark crème de cacao (chocolate liqueur)

1 fl oz blackcurrant schnapps

Method
Shake all ingredients with ice and strain into a chilled Martini glass. Garnish with a couple of floating blackcurrants.

Born Edward Teach in Bristol, England, Black Beard was one of the most fearsome brigands ever to sail the seven seas. He converted a captured French merchant vessel into a 40-gun warship he named *Queen Anne's Revenge* and proceeded to wreak havoc along the Virginia and Carolina coasts and throughout the Caribbean. He was eventually killed and decapitated by Lieutenant Robert Maynard of the Royal Navy on Ocracoke Island, North Carolina, in 1718. It is said that Black Beard once shot his best mate just to remind his crew how psychotic he could be. Not a man to drink Martinis with.

Smartini

2$\frac{1}{2}$ fl oz citron vodka

1 fl oz white crème de cacao (chocolate liqueur)

$\frac{1}{4}$ fl oz sugar syrup

$\frac{3}{4}$ fl oz chilled water (optional)

4 dashes of orange bitters

Method
Shake all ingredients with ice and strain into a chilled Martini glass. Garnish with a few small chocolate pieces in the bottom of the glass.

Orgasm Martini

2¹/₂ fl oz vodka

¹/₂ fl oz triple sec

¹/₂ fl oz white crème de cacao
(chocolate liqueur)

Method
Shake all ingredients with ice and strain into a
chilled Martini glass. Garnish with an orange twist.

Some practitioners of the Asian spiritual
tradition of Tantric sex aim to eliminate
orgasm from sexual intercourse by remaining
for long periods of time in the pre-orgasmic
state. They believe this will lead to orgasmic
feelings spreading out to all conscious
experience. This drink doesn't have quite that
effect, but it does taste very nice.

Midnight Mint

1¹/₂ fl oz Baileys Irish Cream

³/₄ fl oz white crème de cacao
(chocolate liqueur)

³/₄ fl oz green crème de menthe
(peppermint liqueur)

Method
Shake all ingredients with ice and strain into a
chilled Martini glass. Garnish with a dusting of
chocolate powder.

Chocolate Biscuit

1¹/₂ fl oz Cognac

1¹/₂ fl oz dark crème de cacao
(chocolate liqueur)

1¹/₂ fl oz Kahlua (coffee liqueur)

Method
Shake all ingredients with ice and strain into a
chilled Martini glass. Garnish with a sprinkling
of chocolate powder.

A cosmic combo of Cognac and cocoa.
Eating chocolate releases seratonin in the
brain, producing feelings of pleasure and, in
some chocoholics, acts as an aphrodisiac.
But it can also cause acne. Decisions,
decisions.

Chocolate Covered Strawberrytini

2$\frac{1}{2}$ fl oz strawberry vodka

1$\frac{1}{2}$ fl oz white crème de cacao
(chocolate liqueur)

1 strawberry

melted chocolate for dipping

Method
Please note, it's best to prepare the garnish
the day before you invite your friends round
for a chocolate-coated strawberry frenzy.
Dip the strawberry in the melted chocolate
and leave in the fridge to allow the chocolate
to harden. Shake the strawberry vodka and
white crème de cacao with ice and strain into
a chilled Martini glass. Garnish with
aforementioned chocolaty fruit.

Decadent Martini

3 fl oz vodka

1 fl oz amaretto (almond liqueur)

$\frac{1}{2}$ fl oz chambord (raspberry liqueur)

Method
Shake all ingredients with ice and strain into a
chilled Martini glass. Garnish with a toasted
almond or a fresh raspberry—or both if you're
feeling really decadent.

Peppermint Martini

3 fl oz vodka

1 fl oz white crème de menthe
(peppermint liqueur)

Method
Shake all ingredients with ice and strain into a
chilled Martini glass. Garnish with a sprig of
fresh mint.

Raspberry Mochatini

2 fl oz raspberry vodka

³/₄ fl oz dark crème de cacao
(chocolate liqueur)

³/₄ fl oz chambord (raspberry liqueur)

1 fl oz cold espresso coffee

Method
Shake all ingredients with ice and strain into a
chilled Martini glass. Garnish with a fresh
raspberry.

Chocolate Orange Martini

2 fl oz vodka

2 fl oz white crème de cacao
(chocolate liqueur)

1 fl oz triple sec

Method
Shake all ingredients with ice and strain into
a chilled Martini glass. Garnish with a slice
of orange.

Angel's Delight

1 fl oz triple sec

1¹/₂ fl oz gin

1 fl oz double cream

1 fl oz milk

1 dash of grenadine

Method
Shake all ingredients with ice and strain into a
chilled Martini glass. Garnish with a fresh
strawberry.

Grenadine is a pink syrup made from
pomegranates. Here's how to make your
own, starting with 2¹/₄ lb (1 kg) of
pomegranates. Separate the seeds from the
membranes and skin. Cover the seeds with 1
pint (¹/₂ litre) of water and simmer until they
release their juice (about 5 minutes). Pour
through a cheese-cloth layered sieve into a
bowl, pressing remaining juice from the
seeds. Discard the seeds. Measure the
strained pomegranate juice and add an equal
amount of sugar. Pour into a saucepan and
bring to the boil. Reduce heat and simmer for
10 to 15 minutes. Allow it to cool to room
temperature and add red food coloring if
desired. Decant into a stoppered bottle.

Key Lime Martini

1½ fl oz vanilla vodka

1 fl oz lime vodka

½ fl oz freshly squeezed lime juice

½ fl oz sugar syrup

2 scoops vanilla ice cream

Method
Shake all ingredients with ice and strain into a chilled Martini glass. Garnish with a thin slice of lime.

Cocoa Peach Martini

1½ vodka

1 fl oz Malibu

1 fl oz peach schnapps

1½ fl oz cranberry juice

Method
Shake all ingredients with ice and strain into a chilled Martini glass. Garnish with a slice of peach.

Bounty Martini

1½ fl oz vodka

1 fl oz vanilla vodka

1½ fl oz cream of coconut

¼ fl oz sugar syrup

4 dashes of orange bitters

3 fresh strawberries

Method
Muddle the strawberries with the vodka in the base of a shaker. Pour in the cream of coconut, sugar syrup, and the bitters, shake all ingredients with ice and strain into a chilled Martini glass. Garnish with a fresh strawberry.

Black Forest Gateau Martini

2 fl oz vodka

³/₄ fl oz fraise (strawberry liqueur)

³/₄ fl oz chambord (raspberry liqueur)

¹/₄ fl oz crème de cassis
(blackcurrant liqueur)

1 fl oz double cream

Method
Shake all ingredients with ice and strain into a
chilled Martini glass. Garnish with a sprinkling
of chocolate powder. Or you could rim a
chilled Martini glass with chocolate powder
before you start.

Coffee Martini

2¹/₂ fl oz vanilla vodka

1¹/₂ fl oz coffee liqueur

¹/₂ fl oz chilled espresso coffee

Being a sophisticated cocktail drinker, you surely
know the difference between a cappuccino and
a latte but have you ever heard of weasel
coffee? It's a great delicacy from Vietnam where
it is made from coffee beans that have been
eaten and then regurgitated by weasels. True.
The weasels' gastric juices alter the taste of the
beans to produce a coffee that is considered
stronger and smoother.

Method
Shake all ingredients with ice and strain into a
chilled Martini glass. Garnish with a chocolate-
coated coffee bean.

Chocolate Lemontini

1¹/₂ fl oz vodka

1 fl oz white crème de cacao
(chocolate liqueur)

1 fl oz limoncello (lemon liqueur)

Method
Shake all ingredients with ice and strain into a
chilled Martini glass. Garnish with a lemon twist.

Poohtini

2 teaspoons runny honey

2 fl oz Zubrowka (bison grass vodka)

¹/₂ fl oz Krupnik (honey liqueur)

1¹/₂ fl oz cold camomile tea

Method
Stir honey and vodka in the base of a shaker
to combine. Pour in the honey liqueur and
cold tea, shake all ingredients with ice and
strain into a chilled Martini glass. Garnish with
an orange twist.

Alternatini

2 fl oz vodka

1 fl oz white crème de cacao
(chocolate liqueur)

¹/₂ fl oz sweet vermouth

¹/₂ fl oz dry vermouth

Method
Rim a chilled Martini glass with chocolate
powder. Shake the vodka, white crème de
cacao, and two shades of vermouth with ice
and strain into a chilled Martini glass. Garnish
with a piece of chocolate flake.

Vanilla Sensation

2 fl oz vanilla vodka

1 fl oz sour apple liqueur

¹/₂ fl oz dry vermouth

Method
Shake all ingredients with ice and strain into a
chilled Martini glass. Garnish with a thin slice
of floating apple.

Egg Custard Martini

2 fl oz vodka

1$\frac{1}{2}$ fl oz advocaat

$\frac{1}{2}$ fl oz bourbon

$\frac{1}{2}$ fl oz vanilla vodka

$\frac{1}{4}$ fl oz sugar syrup

Method
Shake all ingredients with ice and strain into a chilled Martini glass. Garnish with grated nutmeg.

Custard thickened with starch—what the French call crème patissiere— is known in scientific circles as a non-Newtonian fluid, which means that if it is impacted with sufficient force it behaves more like a solid than a liquid. Consequently, it is possible for a full-grown adult to walk across a swimming pool full of custard without sinking.

Sex & Violets

2$\frac{1}{2}$ fl oz gin

1 fl oz Parfait Amour

Method
Shake all ingredients with ice and strain into a chilled Martini glass. Garnish with an orange twist and float a few violet petals on the drink if you're hoping to get lucky.

Knockout Martini

1 fl oz gin

1 fl oz dry vermouth

1 fl oz Pernod

$^{1}/_{2}$ fl oz white crème de cacao
(chocolate liqueur)

Method
Shake all ingredients with ice and strain into a
chilled Martini glass. Garnish with a
maraschino cherry.

Henri-Louis Pernod opened his distillery
producing France's national drink in 1805.
The original Pernod recipe reached 65% to
75% alcohol and contained the hallucinogen
Arthemisia absinthium, an ingredient that was
eventually banned by the French government
in 1915. Today's anise flavored Pernod is the
aperitif of choice for any self-respecting
Frenchman and is distributed in 150 countries.

Black and White Martini

3 fl oz vanilla vodka

1 fl oz white crème de cacao
(chocolate liqueur)

Method
Shake all ingredients with ice and strain into a
chilled Martini glass. Time to get artistic:
garnish with a stick of licorice or a black and
white licorice candy.

Honey & Marmalade Martini

2 teaspoons runny honey

2 fl oz Scotch whisky

1 fl oz freshly squeezed orange juice

1 fl oz freshly squeezed lemon juice

Method
Stir the honey and Scotch to combine in the
base of a shaker. Pour in the orange and
lemon juice, shake all ingredients with ice
and strain into a chilled Martini glass. Garnish
with an orange twist.

Bees beat their wings over honey in the hive
which helps to drive out its moisture content,
keeping it at a level of between 14% and
18%. As long as it remains under 18%
virtually no organism can multiply to
significant amounts in honey. Also, because
of its high sugar concentration, honey kills
bacteria by plasmolysis. The result? Honey
has been used for centuries for its
antibacterial properties for treating infections.
The ancient Egyptians even used it for
preserving and embalming their dead.

Gingertini

2 fl oz gin

1 fl oz ginger wine

1/2 fl oz dry vermouth

1/4 fl oz sugar syrup

1/2 fl oz chilled water (optional)

Method
Shake all ingredients with ice and
strain into a chilled Martini glass.
Garnish with a piece of stem ginger.

Morning Call

2 fl oz Pernod

1 fl oz cherry brandy

1 fl oz freshly squeezed lemon juice

Start the day as you mean to go on.

Method
Shake all ingredients with ice and strain into a
chilled Martini glass. Garnish with a lemon
twist or a cherry.

Bootleg Martini

1 1/2 fl oz bourbon

1 1/2 fl oz sambuca

1 1/2 fl oz Southern Comfort

Smugglers of illegal booze were called
bootleggers because of their cunning ruse of
tucking bottles into their boots to avoid detection.

Method
Shake all ingredients with ice and strain into a
chilled Martini glass. Garnish with an orange twist.

Almond Joy Martini

2 fl oz vodka

$^1/_2$ fl oz hazelnut liqueur

$^1/_2$ fl oz white crème de cacao (chocolate liqueur)

1 dash of coconut milk

Method
Shake all ingredients with ice and strain into a chilled Martini glass. Garnish with a toasted almond.

Imagination

1 fl oz triple sec

1 fl oz tequila

1 fl oz coconut milk

1 fl oz double cream

Containing both coconut milk and double cream, it doesn't take much imagination to work out that this drink has a rich taste.

Method
Shake all ingredients with ice and strain into a chilled Martini glass. Garnish with an orange twist.

Jelly Beanytini

1$^1/_2$ fl oz white rum

1 fl oz peach schnapps

1 fl oz Malibu

2 dashes of orange bitters

$^1/_2$ fl oz chilled water (optional)

Method
Garnish the drink first by putting a few jelly beans in the bottom of a chilled Martini glass. Shake the remaining ingredients with ice and strain into the glass over the jelly beans. You can drink this without the jelly beans—it tastes just as good.

Chocolate Rum Martini

$1/2$ fl oz dark crème de cacao
(chocolate liqueur)

$1/2$ fl oz crème de menthe
(peppermint liqueur)

$1/2$ fl oz double cream

$1/2$ fl oz milk

1 teaspoon golden rum

Method
Shake all the ingredients except the rum with ice and strain into a chilled Martini glass. Carefully pour the teaspoon of rum so that it floats on the surface of the drink.

Ginger Rogers

3 thin slices of root ginger
(thumb-nail sized)

1 fl oz bourbon

$1/2$ fl oz Teichenne (vanilla schnapps)

$1/2$ fl oz cinnamon schnapps

$1/2$ fl oz ginger wine

$1/2$ fl oz freshly squeezed lime juice

$1/2$ fl oz sugar syrup

Method
Muddle the thinly sliced ginger with bourbon in the base of a shaker. Pour in the vanilla schnapps, cinnamon schnapps, ginger wine, lime juice, and sugar syrup. Shake ingredients with ice and strain into a chilled Martini glass. Garnish with a small piece of stem ginger.

Ginger Rogers was born Virginia McMath in Independence, Missouri, on July 16, 1911. Her first film was *A Night in a Dormitory* in 1929 and four years later she was paired with Fred Astaire in *Flying Down to Rio*. The rest is twinkle-toed history.

Latino Martini

$2 1/2$ fl oz vodka

$1/2$ fl oz Frangelico (hazelnut liqueur)

$1/2$ fl oz white crème de cacao
(chocolate liqueur)

$1/2$ fl oz Baileys Irish Cream

Method
Shake all ingredients with ice and strain into a chilled Martini glass. Garnish with a sprinkling of chocolate powder.

Lazarus

1 fl oz vodka

1 fl oz Kahlua (coffee liqueur)

half fl oz Cognac

1 fl oz chilled espresso coffee

When Lazarus was struck down by a life-threatening illness, his sisters sent for Jesus to come and heal him. But Jesus was delayed on his journey and by the time he arrived Lazarus had already been in his tomb for four days. He told one sister, "I am the resurrection and the life; whoever believes in me, even if he dies, will live, and everyone who lives and believes in me will never die." Lazarus rose from the dead.

Method
Shake all ingredients with ice and strain into a chilled Martini glass. Garnish with a couple of coffee beans.

After Eight Martini

1¹/₂ fl oz vodka

1¹/₂ fl oz white crème de cacao (chocolate liqueur)

³/₄ fl oz white crème de menthe (peppermint liqueur)

Method
Shake all ingredients with ice and strain into a chilled Martini glass. Garnish with a cherry.

Midnight Black Martini

3 fl oz vodka

1 fl oz black sambuca

Method
Shake all ingredients with ice and strain into a chilled Martini glass. Garnish with a cherry.

Choco-Coconutini

1 fl oz vodka

1 fl oz Malibu

1 fl oz dark crème de cacao
(chocolate liqueur)

Method
Shake all ingredients with ice and strain into a
chilled Martini glass. Garnish with a sprinkling
of chocolate powder or an orange twist.

Smooth & Creamytini

2 fl oz golden rum

1 fl oz Malibu

$^1/_4$ fl oz crème de banane
(banana liueur)

$^3/_4$ fl oz double cream

$^3/_4$ fl oz milk

Method
Shake all ingredients with ice and strain into
a chilled Martini glass. Garnish with grated
nutmeg.

Monk's Martini

1 fl oz Frangelico (hazelnut liqueur)

1 fl oz Teichenne (butterscotch schnapps)

$^3/_4$ fl oz Kahlua (coffee liqueur)

1 fl oz double cream

1 fl oz milk

Frangelico, apparently, is an abbreviation of
Fra. Angelico, a hermit monk who gathered
wild hazelnuts in the Piedmont hills in northern
Italy in the 17th century. This popular liqueur
contains cacao, coffee, vanilla, and various
Italian herbs and spices, as well as the
hazelnuts that so captivated Father Angelico.

Method
Shake all ingredients with ice and strain into a
chilled Martini glass. Garnish with grated nutmeg.

Hurricane Martini

1 fl oz gin

1 fl oz white crème de menthe (peppermint liqueur)

1 fl oz sugar syrup

Juice of 1 lemon

Method
Shake all ingredients with ice and strain into a chilled Martini glass. Garnish with a lemon twist.

New Orleans Martini

2¹/₂ fl oz vanilla vodka

1 fl oz Pernod

¹/₂ fl oz dry vermouth

1 dash of Angostura bitters

Method
Shake all ingredients with ice and strain into a chilled Martini glass. Garnish with a fresh sprig of mint.

Topper Martini

1 fl oz Cognac

1 fl oz apricot brandy

1 fl oz white crème de menthe (pepermint liqueur)

2 dashes of Pernod

Method
Shake all ingredients with ice and strain into a chilled Martini glass. Garnish with an orange twist.

Caribou Martini

1¹/₂ fl oz vodka

1¹/₂ fl oz Kahlua (coffee liqueur)

Champagne to top up

Method
Shake the vodka and coffee liqueur with ice and strain into a chilled Champagne flute. Top up with chilled Champagne.

For centuries, caribou have been prized for their milk, meat, and fur by Arctic tribes. The Sami people of Scandinavia call male caribou *sarve*, females *vaya*, and they call castrated males *hierke*. It's a simple operation whereby the animal's testicles are bitten off by a tribesman. I'll just stick with the peanuts, thanks.

Green Jade Martini

1 fl oz gin

1 fl oz green crème de menthe (peppermint liqueur)

¹/₂ fl oz double cream

¹/₂ egg white

Method
Shake all ingredients with ice and strain into a chilled Martini glass. Garnish with a green cherry or a fresh sprig of mint.

Oriental Martini

2 fl oz bourbon

1 fl oz sweet red vermouth

1 fl oz white crème de cacao (chocolate liqueur)

1 fl oz freshly squeezed lime juice

¹/₂ fl oz sugar syrup

Crème de cacao comes in two colors, dark and white, which is actually clear. Both are flavored with cacao beans and often scented with vanilla.

Method
Shake all ingredients with ice and strain into a chilled Martini glass. Garnish with a lime twist.

Velvet Martini

2 fl oz vodka

$^1/_2$ fl oz chambord (raspberry liqueur)

$^1/_2$ fl oz dark crème de cacao (chocolate liqueur)

1 fl oz double cream

Method
Shake all ingredients with ice and strain into a chilled Martini glass. Garnish with a fresh raspberry.

Tarte Tatin Martini

2 fl oz vanilla vodka

$^3/_4$ fl oz Calvados

$^3/_4$ fl oz Cartron (caramel liqueur)

2 fl oz double cream

Tarte Tatin, the upside down apple tart, is the signature dish of the Hotel Tatin in Lamotte-Beuvron, France. Legend has it that it was created by accident in 1889.

Method
There are two shaking stages for this Martini. Shake the vanilla vodka, Calvados, and Cartron with ice and strain into a chilled Martini glass. Next, shake the double cream with ice and pour it carefully over the drink to create a layered effect. Garnish with a sprinkling of powdered cinnamon.

Peanut Butter & Jelly Martini

1$^1/_2$ fl oz raspberry vodka

1 fl oz Frangelico (hazelnut liqueur)

2 fl oz cranberry juice

The first known sighting of peanut butter was in 1890 when George A Bayle Jr. started selling ground peanut paste as a protein supplement for people with no or bad teeth.

Method
Shake all ingredients with ice and strain into a chilled Martini glass. Garnish with a couple of fresh raspberries.

Yahoo!

1 1/2 fl oz vanilla vodka

3 fl oz chocolate milk

Method
Shake all ingredients with ice and strain into a chilled Martini glass. Garnish with a sprinkling of powdered chocolate.

Zabaglione Martini

2 fl oz advocaat

1 fl oz Marsala

1/2 fl oz Cognac

3/4 fl oz freshly squeezed lemon juice

1 fresh egg yolk

Method
Shake all ingredients with ice and strain into a chilled Martini glass. Garnish with a lemon twist.

Here's a tall story about the invention of this classic Italian dessert made from eggs, Marsala wine, and sugar. Apparently, there was a great general called Giovan Paolo Baglione who was busy besieging a fortress in Reggio Emilia when his troops suddenly felt a bit peckish. Most of the locals, understandably, had disappeared with the food when Baglione's army arrived, so he sent some men out foraging. They came back with eggs, wine, honey and herbs, which they made into a frothy soup and, hey presto, they'd created zabaglione.

Chocolate Mint Martini

2 fl oz vodka

1 fl oz white crème de cacao
(chocolate liqueur)

1 fl oz white crème de menthe
(peppermint liqueur)

1/2 fl oz dry vermouth

Method
Shake all ingredients with ice and strain into a chilled Martini glass. Garnish with a sprinkling of chocolate powder or rim the glass with it first.

Saint Moritz

2 fl oz chambord (raspberry liqueur)

1½ fl oz double cream

1½ fl oz milk

Method
Shake all ingredients with ice and strain into a chilled Martini glass. Garnish with a fresh raspberry.

Rhubarb & Custard Martini

2 fl oz gin

1½ fl oz advocaat

1½ fl oz syrup from canned rhubarb

Method
Shake all ingredients with ice and strain into a chilled Martini glass. Garnish with a dusting of grated nutmeg.

Advocaat is a rich and creamy blend of egg yolk, aromatic spirits, sugar, brandy, and vanilla from Holland. It was first made by Dutch settlers in South America, who mixed an equally thick drink using the whipped flesh of avocados. Back home in Holland, without avocados to hand, it was found that whipped egg yolks make a reasonable substitute. This is why advocaat comes from the Dutch for avocado even though there are no avocados in it.

Bourbon Milk Punch

1 fl oz bourbon

2 fl oz double cream

1 fl oz milk

$^1/_2$ fl oz sugar syrup

1 teaspoon Galliano

Method
Shake all ingredients with ice and strain into a chilled Martini glass. Garnish with a sprinkling of grated nutmeg.

Butterscotch Martini

2 fl oz vodka

1 fl oz butterscotch schnapps

1 fl oz white crème de cacao (chocolate liqueur)

Method
Shake all ingredients with ice and strain into a chilled Martini glass. Garnish with butterscotch chips.

Shahad Martini

$1^1/_2$ fl oz date-infused golden rum

1 fl oz Krupnik (honey liqueur)

$^1/_2$ fl oz freshly squeezed lime juice

$^1/_4$ fl oz lime cordial

4-inch stick of lemon grass to garnish

This spicy little number was created by the talented mixologist, Douglas Ankrah for the Red Fort Indian restaurant in London. Lemon grass, sometimes known as fever grass, is commonly used in teas, soups, and curries. It is also used in perfumes and mosquito repellents.

Method
Shake all ingredients with ice and strain into a chilled Martini glass. Garnish with a lemon twist.

Caramel Martini

2 fl oz vodka

2 fl oz butterscotch schnapps

Method
Shake all ingredients with ice and strain into a chilled Martini glass. Garnish with a dusting of chocolate powder.

Mint Martini

1 1/2 fl oz vodka

1 1/2 fl oz white crème de cacao (chocolate liqueur)

1/2 fl oz crème de menthe (peppermint liqueur)

Method
Shake all ingredients with ice and strain into a chilled Martini glass. Garnish with a sprig of fresh mint.

In Greek mythology, Minthe (also known as Menthe, Mentha, and Mintho) was a nymph of the river Cocytus, the river of wailing, in the underworld. She was dazzled by Hades' golden chariot and was about to be seduced by him when Queen Persephone stepped in and transformed her into a mint plant. Which is handy, considering she was called Minthe anyway.

Snowball Martini

1 fl oz gin

1/2 fl oz Parfait Amour

1/2 fl oz white crème de menthe (peppermint liqueur)

1/2 fl oz Pernod

1/2 fl oz double cream

Parfait Amour is a light purple curacao flavored with rose petals, vanilla and almonds, produced in the Burgundy region of France by Joseph Cartron. Ironically, Parfait Amour (or Perfect Love) was also the favorite drink of an ex-girlfriend of mine. The signs were all there, I just couldn't see them.

Method
Shake all ingredients with ice and strain into a chilled Martini glass. Garnish with a lemon twist.

Road Runner

2 fl oz vodka

1 fl oz amaretto (almond liqueur)

1 fl oz coconut milk

Method
Shake all ingredients with ice and strain into a chilled Martini glass. Garnish with a pinch of grated nutmeg.

Sorry to shatter any childhood illusions, but the greater roadrunner (*Geococcyx California*) can run at speeds of up to 15 mph (24 kph). This is remarkable for a bird that stands little more than a foot tall, but the coyote can run at speeds of up to 40 mph (64 kph), which kind of undermines the whole premise of Chuck Jones' classic cartoon series. Martini philosophy time: Chuck Jones once said, "Wile E (Coyote) is my reality, Bugs Bunny is my goal."

Tiramisu Martini

2$^1/_2$ fl oz Cognac

$^1/_2$ fl oz dark crème de cacao (chocolate liqueur)

$^1/_2$ fl oz coffee liqueur

$^1/_2$ fl oz milk

$^1/_2$ fl oz double cream

1 teaspoon mascarpone

1 fresh egg yolk

Method
Shake all ingredients with ice and strain into a chilled Martini glass. To garnish, dust with chocolate powder.

131

Ninitchka

3 fl fl oz vodka

2 fl oz white crème de cacao
(chocolate liqueur)

1 fl oz freshly squeezed lemon juice

Method
Shake all ingredients with ice and strain into a
chilled Martini glass. Garnish with a lemon
twist. If you were to add a couple of dashes
of grenadine you would end up with another
(pinkish) Russian-sounding Martini called a
Kretchma.

Turkish Delight Martini

Method
Pour the vodka and honey into the base of a shaker and stir to combine.
Pour in the remaining ingredients, shake with ice and strain into a
chilled Martini glass. Garnish with a piece of Turkish Delight
on a cocktail stick.

2 fl oz vanilla vodka

$\frac{1}{2}$ fl oz white crème de
cacao (chocolate liqueur)

2 teaspoons runny honey

1 dash of rose water

1 fl oz chilled water

$\frac{1}{2}$ a fresh egg white

Turkish Delight, also known as "lokum," is a confection made
from sugar and starch flavored with rosewater or lemon, dusted
with sugar and sometimes containing pistachios, hazelnuts, or
walnuts. It is not limited to Turkey, being very popular
throughout the Middle East, Greece, and the Balkan countries.

Alexander

1$\frac{1}{2}$ fl oz gin

1$\frac{1}{2}$ fl oz white crème de cacao
(chocolate liqueur)

1$\frac{1}{2}$ fl oz double cream

Method
Shake ingredients with ice and strain into a chilled
Martini glass. Garnish with grated nutmeg.

This was a firm favorite during Prohibition
(1920-1933). It proved an effective way to
disguise the quality of moonshine gin, which
was often distilled in bathtubs. According to a
bar book written at the time, "The (bathtub) gin
is aged about the length of time it takes to get
from the bathroom where it is made to the front
porch where the cocktail party is in progress."

Vanilla Twist Martini

3 fl oz vanilla vodka

$^1/_2$ fl oz triple sec

$^1/_2$ fl oz dry vermouth

Vanilla was brought to Europe from Mexico by the Spanish Conquistadors. Today, the largest vanilla producer is Madagascar and the Coco-Cola Corporation is the world's largest customer of natural vanilla extract.

Method
Shake all ingredients with ice and strain into a chilled Martini glass. Garnish with an orange twist.

Eager Beaver Martini

1$^1/_2$ fl oz vodka

1$^1/_2$ fl oz Kahlua (coffee liqueur)

$^1/_2$ fl oz triple sec

Method
Shake all ingredients with ice and strain into a chilled Martini glass. Garnish with an orange twist.

Parma Violet Martini

1$^1/_2$ fl oz vodka

$^1/_4$ fl oz peach schnapps

$^1/_2$ fl oz freshly squeezed lemon juice

$^3/_4$ fl oz Parfait Amour

$^1/_4$ fl oz sugar syrup

4 dashes of orange bitters

Method
Shake all ingredients with ice and strain into a chilled Martini glass. Garnish with a few violet petals floating on the surface of the drink.

Vodka Espresso

2¹/₂ fl oz vodka

1¹/₂ fl oz cold espresso coffee

¹/₂ fl oz Kahlua (coffee liqueur)

¹/₄ fl oz sugar syrup

Method
Shake all ingredients with ice and strain into a chilled Martini glass. Garnish with a couple of coffee beans.

Buff Martini

2¹/₂ fl oz vodka

¹/₂ fl oz Kahlua (coffee liqueur)

¹/₂ fl oz Baileys Irish Cream

Method
Shake all ingredients with ice and strain into a chilled Martini glass. Garnish with a couple of coffee beans.

Dazed and Infused

3 fl oz vanilla vodka

¹/₂ fl oz Baileys Irish Cream

Method
Shake all ingredients with ice and strain into a chilled Martini glass. Garnish with a sprinkling of powdered cinnamon.

Whip Martini

1 fl oz Pernod

1 fl oz Cognac

1 fl oz dry vermouth

1 fl oz triple sec

Method
Shake all ingredients with ice and strain into a chilled Martini glass. Garnish with an orange twist.

White Satin

1 1/2 fl oz Kahlua (coffee liqueur)

1 1/2 fl oz Galliano

1 fl oz milk

1/2 fl oz double cream

This rich, creamy Martini feels as smooth as satin, hence the name.

Method
Shake all ingredients with ice and strain into a chilled Martini glass. Garnish with a chocolate-coated coffee bean.

Tootsie Roll Martini

3 fl oz vodka

1/2 fl oz Grand Marnier

1/2 fl oz chocolate liqueur

Method
Shake all ingredients with ice and strain into a chilled Martini glass. Garnish with an orange twist.

Xena Martini

2 1/2 fl oz honey vodka

1/2 fl oz bison grass vodka

1 teaspoon Lillet Blanc

Xena, Warrior Princess was played in the popular television series by New Zealander Lucy Lawless. Anyway, she was chosen by *People* magazine as one of the 50 Most Beautiful People in the World in 1997.

Method
Shake all ingredients with ice and strain into a chilled Martini glass. I've even heard it suggested that a Xena Martini can be garnished with a spear of pickled asparagus, but I'd prefer it with no garnish. Call me old-fashioned but ...

Chocolate Martini

3 fl oz vodka

¹/₂ fl oz white crème de cacao
(chocolate liqueur)

Method
Shake all ingredients with ice and strain into a chilled Martini glass. Garnish with a sprinkling of chocolate powder or a chocolate flake.

Yankee Prince

1¹/₂ fl oz Pernod

1¹/₂ fl oz apricot brandy

1¹/₂ fl oz yellow Chartreuse

Method
Shake all ingredients with ice and strain into a chilled Martini glass. Garnish with an orange twist.

Easter Martini

4 pods green cardamom

2¹/₂ fl oz vanilla vodka

1 fl oz white crème de cacao
(chocolate liqueur)

¹/₄ fl oz sugar syrup

Method
Remove outer shells of cardamom and crush the pods in the base of a shaker with the vanilla vodka. Pour in the crème de cacao and sugar syrup, shake all ingredients with ice and strain into a chilled Martini glass. Garnish with a sprinkling of chocolate powder.

Cardamom is the dried unopened fruit of the perennial *Elettaria cardamomum*. It is one of the most popular spices throughout the Arab world, where cardamom coffee is a symbol of hospitality and prestige. In Iceland it's called kardamomma!

Christmas Martini

3 fl oz gin

$^1/_2$ fl oz dry vermouth

$^1/_4$ fl oz peppermint schnapps

Miniature candy cane to garnish

Method

Shake all ingredients with ice and strain into a chilled Martini glass. Garnish with a miniature candy cane. Well, it is Christmas.

We all know candy cane as a traditional Christmas confectionary. Originally, it was an all-white, straight candy stick but it has evolved over the years. A choirmaster at Cologne cathedral in Germany, who was in the habit of giving candy to children at his services, is credited with creating the cane shape when he, allegedly, bent straight candy sticks to represent a shepherd's staff. An unnamed Protestant in 1870s Indiana is thought to have bent these candy sticks into a J shape to represent Jesus. He also added the red stripes to represent the blood of Christ, while the white stripes signify his purity.

Zingy Ginger Martini

$2^1/_2$ fl oz citron vodka

1 fl oz ginger wine

1 fl oz chilled water (optional)

1 teaspoon freshly squeezed lemon juice

Method

Shake all ingredients with ice and strain into a chilled Martini glass. Garnish with a lemon twist.

alternatinis

Mexico City

1¹/₂ fl oz tequila

1 fl oz Grand Marnier

¹/₂ fl oz freshly squeezed lime juice

¹/₂ fl oz cranberry juice

¹/₄ fl oz sugar syrup

Method
Shake all ingredients with ice and strain into a chilled Martini glass. Garnish with a lime twist.

Xanthia Martini

1¹/₂ fl oz gin

1¹/₂ fl oz Yellow Chartreuse

1¹/₂ fl oz cherry brandy

Method
Shake all ingredients with ice and strain into a chilled Martini glass. Garnish with a cherry impaled on a cocktail stick.

Bikinitini (or Teeny Weeny Bikinitini)

2¹/₂ fl oz vodka

1 fl oz white rum

¹/₂ fl oz freshly squeezed lemon juice

¹/₂ fl oz milk

1 dash of sugar syrup

Method
Shake all ingredients with ice and strain into a chilled Martini glass. Garnish with a lemon twist.

The women of ancient Rome are known to have worn bikini-esque garments, and female Greek athletes wearing similar are depicted on urns dating back to 1,400 BCE. The modern bikini was "invented" in Paris in 1946 by engineer Louis Reard. In his view, "A bikini is not a bikini unless it can be pulled through a wedding ring." He named his design after Bikini Atoll, the site of nuclear testing, because he said the excitement it would cause among men would be similar to the detonation of an atomic bomb. Despite its ancient heritage, it took Brigitte Bardot's film, *And God Created Woman*, in 1957 for the bikini to become acceptable in the US.

Incognito

2 fl oz Cognac

1½ fl oz dry vermouth

1 fl oz apricot brandy

3 dashes of Angostura bitters

Method
Shake all ingredients with ice and strain into a chilled Martini glass. Garnish with an orange twist.

Blackthorn English Martini

1½ fl oz sloe gin

1 fl oz gin

1 fl oz sweet vermouth

3 dashes of orange bitters

1 fl oz chilled water

Method
Shake all ingredients with ice and strain into a Martini glass. Garnish with an orange twist.

Bootlegger Martini

3 fl oz gin

$^1/_2$ fl oz Southern Comfort

Method
Shake all ingredients with ice and strain into
a chilled Martini glass. Garnish with an
orange twist.

During Prohibition (1920-1933) the US
Temperance movement showed how
intemperate it could be. It was suggested at
one point that poisoned alcoholic beverages
should be distributed by bootleggers on the
grounds that several thousand deaths would
be a price worth paying for stamping out
drinking for good. Other suggestions for
those who drank included being placed in
bottle-shaped cages in public squares and
being hung by the tongue beneath an
aeroplane and flown over the country.

Float Like a Butterfly

$1^1/_2$ fl oz dry vermouth

$1^1/_2$ fl oz sweet vermouth

1 fl oz Dubonnet red

1 fl oz freshly squeezed orange juice

Method
Shake all ingredients with ice and strain into a
chilled Martini glass. Garnish with an orange
twist. Sure, this one contains alcohol but no hard
liquor, which means it doesn't sting like a bee.

Muhammad Ali, previously Cassius Marcellus
Clay, aka the Louisville Lip, was born in
Louisville, Kentucky in 1942. His boxing career
extended to 61 bouts including 37 knockouts.
None have been more celebrated than *The
Rumble in the Jungle*, his epic encounter with
George Foreman in Zaire. Going into the fight
as a 3-1 underdog, Ali perfected his "rope-on-
a-dope" tactic whereby he allowed Foreman to
pummel him on the ropes for the first seven
rounds before knocking his exhausted
opponent out in the eighth.

Ivy Club Martini

3 fl oz gin

1 fl oz amaretto (almond liqueur)

1 fl oz freshly squeezed lime juice

Method
Shake all ingredients with ice and strain into a chilled Martini glass. Garnish with a lime twist.

When the Ivy Club opened in 1879 it was the first of 10 eating clubs at Princeton University. All but one of these private clubs occupy large mansion houses on Prospect Avenue, and five of them—University Cottage Club, Cap and Gown Club, Tiger Inn, Princeton Tower Club, and the Ivy Club—select their members through a process called bicker. It occurs each spring semester when applicants are grilled in interviews or subjected to madcap games and crazy antics, depending on the club. The eating clubs are the students' answer to Princeton's traditional ban on secret societies, in force until as recently as the 1980s.

Busy Bee Sting Martini

2 fl oz brandy

1 fl oz vodka

1 fl oz crème de menthe (peppermint liqueur)

$^1/_2$ fl oz Krupnik (honey liqueur)

Method
Shake all ingredients with ice and strain into a chilled Martini glass. Garnish with a fresh mint sprig.

It is a misconception that bees can sting only once, and then die, because the barbs in their stings get lodged in the victim, causing their abdomens to tear. In fact, the barbed sting was designed for inter-bee combat and can be withdrawn quite safely from another bee's exoskeleton. The damage occurs to bees only when they sting mammals. Queen bees, of course, have smooth stingers and can blissfully sting to their hearts' content.

Sidecar Martini

1 fl oz vodka

1 fl oz brandy

1 fl oz triple sec

$1/2$ fl oz freshly squeezed lemon juice

Method
Shake all ingredients with ice and strain into a chilled Martini glass. Garnish with a lemon twist.

Dutch Breakfast Martini

$1^1/2$ fl oz gin

$1^1/2$ fl oz advocaat

1 fl oz freshly squeezed lemon juice

$1/4$ fl oz sugar syrup

1 dash of Galliano

Galliano is a yellow liqueur flavored with star anise and vanilla. It was created in 1896 by an Italian distiller called Arturo Vaccari and is named after Maggiore Galliano, an Italian hero of the East African war in the 19th century.

Method
Shake all ingredients with ice and strain into a chilled Martini glass. Garnish with an orange twist.

Carpano Martini

$1^1/2$ fl oz sloe gin

1 fl oz Punt e Mes

$1/4$ fl oz freshly squeezed lime juice

$1/4$ fl oz sugar syrup

Method
Shake all ingredients with ice and strain into a chilled Martini glass. Garnish with a lime twist.

Punt e Mes was originally a mix of one and a half "points" of dark bitters with white vermouth. Nowadays it is a premixed red vermouth brand from the Carpano company. Vermouth was allegedly invented by Antonio Benedetto Carpano in Turin in 1786 as a sweeter alternative to the locally produced red wine and was said to be more suitable for the ladies.

KGB

2 fl oz gin

1 fl oz kümmel (caraway seed, cumin, and fennel liqueur)

1 fl oz apricot brandy

$\frac{1}{2}$ fl oz freshly squeezed lemon juice

Method
Shake all ingredients with ice and strain into a Martini glass. Garnish with a lemon twist.

The KGB, the Russian State Security Committee, operated from 1954 until 1991. It was disbanded as the man in charge, Colonel-General Vladimir Kryuchkov, was found to have used KGB resources in an attempted coup to overthrow President Mikhail Gorbachev. It has been replaced by the FSB, which is not discernibly different. Russian President Vladimir Putin started his career in the KGB.

Chill-Out Martini

$1\frac{1}{2}$ fl oz orange vodka

1 fl oz Baileys Irish Cream

$1\frac{1}{2}$ fl oz Malibu

$1\frac{1}{2}$ fl oz freshly squeezed orange juice

Method
Shake all ingredients with ice and strain into a chilled Martini glass. Garnish with a thin slice of pineapple.

Double Vision Martini

3 fl oz vodka

1 fl oz triple sec

1 fl oz freshly pressed pineapple juice

Method
Shake all ingredients with ice and strain into a chilled Martini glass. Garnish with a thin slice of pineapple.

Pichuncho Martini

2$\frac{1}{2}$ fl oz Pisco (clear
South American brandy)

1$\frac{1}{2}$ fl oz sweet vermouth

$\frac{1}{4}$ fl oz sugar syrup

Pichuncho, a mix of Pisco and vermouth, is a
very popular drink in Chile.

Method
Shake all ingredients with ice and strain into a
chilled Martini glass. Garnish with an orange twist.

Venus Martini

6 fresh raspberries

2$\frac{1}{2}$ fl oz gin

1 fl oz triple sec

$\frac{1}{4}$ fl oz sugar syrup

4 dashes of orange bitters (optional)

Method
Muddle the raspberries with the gin in the
base of a shaker. Pour in the triple sec, sugar
syrup, and bitters, shake with ice and strain
into a chilled Martini glass. Garnish with a
fresh raspberry.

Clear-Coin Martini

1 fl oz vodka

1 fl oz Campari

2 fl oz freshly squeezed orange juice

Method
Swirl the Campari around a chilled Martini
glass and discard (the Campari). Shake the
vodka and orange juice with ice, strain into
the glass and garnish with an orange twist.

Sloe Gin Martini

2¹/₂ fl oz sloe gin

1 fl oz dry vermouth

1 dash of Angostura bitters

Method
Shake all ingredients with ice and strain into a
chilled Martini glass. Garnish with a lemon twist.

Sloe gin is infused with the small, sour, blue-
black fruit of the blackthorn, otherwise known
as the sloe berry. To make sloe gin, you will
need ripe berries, which are traditionally
picked in late October to early November.
Prick each berry with a fork and half-fill a jar.
For each 1 pint (¹/₂ liter) of sloes add 3¹/₂ oz
(100 grams) of ultrafine sugar and top up the
jar with gin. Seal the jar and turn it several
times to mix, then store in a cool, dark place.
Repeat the turning every day for two weeks,
then each week for about three months. Pour
off the infused gin and discard the berries,
then decant the gin into clean containers and
leave to stand for another week.

Remy Martini

2 fl oz Remy Martin Cognac

³/₄ fl oz triple sec

¹/₄ fl oz sugar syrup

1¹/₂ fl oz freshly
pressed pineapple juice

2 dashes of Angostura bitters

Method
Shake all ingredients with ice and strain into a
chilled Martini glass. Garnish with an orange twist.

Negroni Martini

1 fl oz gin

1 fl oz sweet vermouth

1 fl oz Campari

Method
Shake all ingredients with ice and strain into a
chilled Martini glass. Garnish with an orange
twist.

Cucumber Martini

2 fl oz Zubrowka (bison grass vodka)

1 fl oz vodka

$^1/_2$ fl oz sugar syrup

2 inches (5 cm) of peeled chopped cucumber

Method

Muddle the cucumber with the Zubrowka in the base of a shaker. Pour in the standard vodka and sugar syrup, shake with ice and strain into a chilled Martini glass. Garnish with a strip of cucumber peel.

DNA

1$^1/_2$ fl oz gin

$^3/_4$ fl oz apricot brandy

1 fl oz freshly squeezed lemon juice

$^1/_4$ fl oz sugar syrup

4 dashes of orange bitters (optional)

DNA (or deoxyribonucleic acid) contains the genetic instructions for all forms of cellular life. DNA profiling to help catch criminals was developed in 1984 by Alec Jeffreys at the University of Leicester in England. Colin Pitchfork, who was convicted of the Enderby murders in Leicestershire, was the first criminal to be ensnared by this breakthrough development.

Method

Shake all ingredients with ice and strain into a chilled Martini glass. Garnish with an orange twist.

Playmate Martini

Method
Shake all ingredients with ice and strain into a chilled Martini glass. Garnish with a lemon twist.

1 fl oz Zubrowka (bison grass vodka)

1 fl oz Krupnik (honey liqueur)

1 fl oz vodka

1 fl oz freshly pressed apple juice

Detroit Martini

2 fl oz vodka

$1/2$ fl oz sugar syrup

6 fresh mint leaves

Method
Shake all ingredients with ice and strain into a chilled Martini glass. Garnish with a sprig of fresh mint.

Diego Martini

3 fl oz vodka

$1/2$ fl oz tequila

$1/2$ fl oz freshly squeezed orange juice

Method
Shake all ingredients with ice and strain into a chilled Martini glass. Garnish with an orange twist.

Diego Armando Maradonna, considered by many to be the world's greatest ever soccer player, was born in 1960 in Villa Fiorito, a shantytown on the southern outskirts of Buenos Aires. Speaking on his chat show about the infamous Hand of God episode, where he illegally used his hand to score a goal against England in the 1986 World Cup, he confessed, "I was waiting for my team mates to embrace me ... I told them, 'Come hug me or the referee isn't going to allow it.'" His second goal in the match, when he ran half the length of the pitch through five England players, was voted Goal of the Century in a poll conducted by FIFA, football's international governing body.

Double S & M Martini

2¹/₂ fl oz vodka

1 fl oz sambuca

¹/₂ fl oz crème de menthe
(peppermint liqueur)

Method
Shake all ingredients with ice and strain into a
Martini glass.

Carlton Cocktail

2 fl oz Canadian whisky

1 fl oz orange curacao

1 fl oz freshly squeezed lemon juice

Method
Shake all ingredients with ice and strain into a
chilled Martini glass. Garnish with a lemon twist.

Elderflower Martini

2¹/₂ fl oz Zubrowka (bison grass vodka)

¹/₂ fl oz dry vermouth

1¹/₂ fl oz elderflower cordial

Method
Shake all ingredients with ice and strain into a
chilled Martini glass. Garnish with a lemon twist.

Russian River Martini

2 fl oz vodka

¹/₂ fl oz Drambuie

1¹/₂ fl oz cranberry juice

¹/₄ fl oz freshly squeezed lemon juice

¹/₄ fl oz sugar syrup

Method
Shake all ingredients with ice and strain into a
chilled Martini glass. Garnish with a lemon twist.

Russian River in Sonoma is one of California's
prime winegrowing regions. Relatively cool
and with frequent fog rolling in off the Pacific
ocean, it is particularly well suited to making
still and sparkling wines from the Burgundian
Chardonnay and Pinot Noir grape varieties.
The river is named after Russian trappers who
explored it in the early 19th century, when
Russia maintained trading colonies along the
northern coast of California.

Emerald Martini

3 fl oz vodka

1 fl oz dry vermouth

$^1/_4$ fl oz green chartreuse

Method
Shake all ingredients with ice and strain into a
chilled Martini glass. Garnish with a lemon twist.

Golden Nugget Martini

3 fl oz vodka

$^1/_2$ fl oz Frangelico (hazelnut liqueur)

Method
Shake all ingredients with ice and strain into a
chilled Martini glass. Garnish with an orange twist.

The Golden Nugget casino in Las Vegas, built
in 1946, has on display in its lobby the world's
largest golden nugget. *The Hand of Faith*, as
it is known, weighs 60 lb (27.2 kg) and is 19
inches (46 cm) in length. It was found near a
region called the Golden Triangle in Australia.

Love Martini

2 fl oz gin

1 fl oz green curacao

Method
Shake all ingredients with ice and strain into a
chilled Martini glass. Garnish with a lemon twist.

Jacktini

1 fl oz bourbon

1 fl oz Mandarine Napoleon
(tangerine liqueur)

1¹/₂ fl oz freshly squeezed lemon juice

¹/₂ fl oz sugar syrup

Method
Shake all ingredients with ice and strain
into a chilled Martini glass. Garnish with
an orange twist.

Brazen Martini

3 fl oz vodka

¹/₂ fl oz Parfait Amour (rose petal,
vanilla, and almond flavored liqueur)

Method
Shake all ingredients with ice and strain into a
chilled Martini glass. Garnish with a couple of
floating blackberries or blueberries.

English Martini

2¹/₂ fl oz gin

1 fl oz elderflower cordial

¹/₂ fl oz sugar syrup

1 sprig of rosemary

Method
Muddle the rosemary with gin in the base of
a shaker. Pour in the elderflower cordial and
sugar syrup, shake with ice and strain into a
chilled Martini glass. Garnish with a small
sprig of rosemary.

Native to the Mediterranean region, rosemary
is an evergreen member of the mint family. Its
Latin name, *Rosmarinus*, means "dew of the
sea." According to legend, rosemary is good
for improving memory and has been widely
used as a symbol of remembrance. In a light-
hearted moment in Shakespeare's Hamlet,
Ophelia quips, "There's rosemary, that's for
remembrance."

Gelardi Martini

2¹/₂ fl oz gin

1 fl oz triple sec

1 or 2 teaspoons orange marmalade (according to taste)

1 dash of freshly squeezed lemon juice

Sometimes called the Breakfast Martini, this one was created by Salvatore Calabrese at The Lanesborough Hotel in London.

Method
Shake all ingredients with ice and strain into a chilled Martini glass. You'll have to shake this one particularly vigorously in order to combine the marmalade. Garnish with a lemon twist.

Mystique Martini

2 fl oz Scotch whisky

1 fl oz Tuaca liqueur (vanilla citrus liqueur)

³/₄ fl oz chambord (raspberry liqueur)

Method
Shake all ingredients with ice and strain into a chilled Martini glass. Garnish with a couple of fresh raspberries.

Tuaca is a sweet, sticky Italian liqueur flavored with vanilla and citrus fruits, produced by the Tuoni family in Livorno, Tuscany. The recipe supposedly dates back to the Renaissance and was created for Lorenzo di Piero de Medici, ruler of the Florentine Republic. Supremely gifted in the manly pursuits of jousting and hunting and the head of a group of brilliant scholars and poets, he rejoiced in the nickname *Lorenzo the Magnificent*.

Parrothead Martini

3 fl oz tequila

$\frac{1}{2}$ fl oz triple sec

$\frac{1}{2}$ fl oz freshly squeezed lime juice

Method
Shake all ingredients with ice and strain into a chilled Martini glass. Garnish with a lime twist.

Green Fairy

1 fl oz absinthe

1 fl oz freshly
squeezed lemon juice

1 fl oz sugar syrup

1 fl oz chilled water

$\frac{1}{2}$ a fresh egg white

2 dashes of Angostura bitters

Method
Shake all ingredients with ice and strain into a chilled Martini glass. Garnish with a lemon twist.

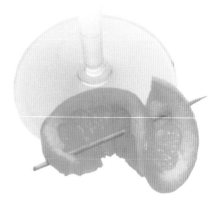

Gumdrop Martini

2 fl oz lemon rum

1 fl oz vodka

$^1/_2$ fl oz Southern Comfort

$^1/_2$ fl oz freshly pressed lemon juice

1 dash of dry vermouth

Method
Shake all ingredients with ice and strain into a
chilled Martini glass. Garnish with a lemon twist.

Julep Martini

8 fresh mint leaves

3 fl oz bourbon

$^1/_2$ fl oz sugar syrup

$^3/_4$ fl oz chilled water

Method
Muddle the mint leaves with the bourbon in
the base of a shaker. Add the sugar syrup
and chilled water, shake all ingredients with
ice and strain into a chilled Martini glass.
Garnish with a fresh mint leaf.

The official drink of the Kentucky Derby, the
super-refreshing Mint Julep originated in
Virginia. In 1803, John Davis, an English tutor
working in the grand houses of the southern
plantations, wrote that a julep is "a dram of
spirituous liquor that has mint in it, taken by
Virginians of a morning." Those mornings
must just fly past.

Hip Cat Martini

3 fl oz blackberry vodka

$^1/_2$ fl oz dry vermouth

$^1/_2$ fl oz sweet vermouth

$^1/_2$ fl oz triple sec

The words "hip," "hep," and "hipcat" derive from the Wolof language spoken by West Africans who were kidnapped and enslaved by Europeans and Americans. In Wolof, the word "hepicat" translates as "one who has his eyes open."

Method
Shake all ingredients with ice and strain into a chilled Martini glass. Garnish with a fresh blackberry.

Hoosier Martini

2 fl oz Zubrowka (bison grass vodka)

1 fl oz white rum

$^1/_2$ fl oz dry vermouth

Method
Shake all ingredients with ice and strain into a chilled Martini glass. Garnish with a lemon twist.

"Hoosier" is the nickname for someone from the State of Indiana, though no one really knows why. One of the favorite stories is that a contractor named Samuel Hoosier helped to build a canal on the Ohio River in 1825. His workers, who were predominantly from Indiana, were known as "Hoosier's men." Alternatively, it derives from "hoozer" an old English word from Cumberland in the north of the country meaning a high hill or hill dweller.

Black Ice Martini

2 fl oz vodka

2 fl oz black sambuca

$^1/_4$ fl oz crème de menthe (peppermint liqueur)

Method
Shake all ingredients with ice and strain into a chilled Martini glass. Garnish with an orange twist.

Imperial

1½ fl oz gin

1½ fl oz dry vermouth

1 fl oz maraschino liqueur
(cherry liqueur)

3 dashes of Angostura bitters

Method
Shake all ingredients with ice and strain into a
chilled Martini glass. Garnish with a green olive.

Bronx Terrace Martini

3 fl oz gin

1 fl oz freshly squeezed lime juice

$^1/_2$ fl oz dry vermouth

Method
Shake all ingredients with ice and strain into a chilled Martini glass. Garnish with a cherry.

The Bronx is the only one of New York City's five boroughs to be part of the US mainland, being separated from the island of Manhattan by the Harlem River. Home to 1.3 million New Yorkers, it is named after Jonas Bronck, a Swedish-Dutch sea captain who owned a 500-acre farm in the area in the 1640s. Famous Bronxites include Woody Allen, Tony Curtis, Linda Lovelace, Al Pacino, John Gotti, and hip hop music pioneers Grandmaster Flash and Grandmaster Melle Mel.

Fine and Dandy

2 fl oz gin

1 fl oz triple sec

1 fl oz freshly squeezed lime juice

$^3/_4$ fl oz sugar syrup

4 dashes of Angostura bitters

Method
Shake all ingredients with ice and strain into a chilled Martini glass. Garnish with a lime twist.

Jet Black Martini

3 fl oz gin

$^1/_2$ fl oz black sambuca

$^1/_4$ fl oz sweet vermouth

Method
Shake all ingredients with ice and strain into a chilled Martini glass. Garnish with a lemon twist.

Hair Raiser Martini

1 fl oz brandy

1 fl oz Pernod

1 fl oz triple sec

Method
Shake all ingredients with ice and strain into a chilled Martini glass. Garnish with an orange twist.

Whiskey Martini

3 fl oz bourbon

1 fl oz orange curacao

2 dashes of Angostura bitters

Method
Shake all ingredients with ice and strain into a chilled Martini glass. Garnish with a cherry.

Jade

2¹/₂ fl oz golden rum

¹/₂ fl oz blue curacao

¹/₂ fl oz freshly squeezed lime juice

1 teaspoon sugar syrup

Despite its ornamental value, jade is an incredibly tough stone that was first used for weapons and axe heads before metals took off. It is also the official gemstone of British Columbia, which has substantial jade deposits in the Lillooet and Cassiar regions.

Method
Shake all ingredients with ice and strain into a chilled Martini glass. Garnish with an orange twist.

Picca Martini

2¹/₂ fl oz Scotch whisky

1 fl oz Punt e Mes

1 fl oz Galliano

Method
Shake all ingredients with ice and strain into a chilled Martini glass. Garnish with a cherry.

Chelsea Sidecar

1¹/₂ fl oz gin

1 fl oz triple sec

1¹/₄ fl oz freshly squeezed lime juice

¹/₄ fl oz freshly squeezed lemon juice

1 fl oz sugar syrup

Chelsea Football Club, an English soccer team, was founded on March 14, 1905, at The Rising Sun pub in Fulham, southwest London. It was bought by Russian billionaire Roman Abramovich in June 2003, winning the league championship the following season.

Method
Shake all ingredients with ice and strain into a chilled Martini glass. Garnish with a lemon twist.

Lava Lamp Martini

3 fl oz vodka

¹/₂ fl oz chambord (raspberry liqueur)

1 teaspoon runny honey

Method
Stir the honey and chambord together in a mixing glass. Shake the vodka with ice and strain into a chilled Martini glass. Slowly pour the honey and chambord mixture onto the surface of the drink.

Mule's Hind Leg Martini

1 fl oz gin

1 fl oz Benedictine

1 fl oz Calvados

1 fl oz apricot brandy

$^1/_2$ fl oz maple syrup

Method
Shake all ingredients with ice and strain into a chilled Martini glass. Garnish with an orange twist.

London Martini

3 fl oz gin

2 dashes of maraschino

2 dashes of orange bitters

$^1/_4$ dash of sugar syrup

Method
Shake all ingredients with ice and strain into a chilled Martini glass. Garnish with a lemon twist.

London is an Alpha world city, according to the Globalization and World Cities Study Group (GaWC) at Loughborough University in Leicestershire, England. Ranking cities based on their provision of "advanced producer services" such as accountancy and advertising by international firms, GaWC considers the other Alpha world cities to be New York, Paris, and Tokyo. Just behind them, scoring fewer points, are Chicago, Frankfurt, Hong Kong, Los Angeles, Milan, and Singapore. Beta world cities include San Francisco, Sydney, Brussels, and Moscow, while Gamma cities include Amsterdam, Boston, Bangkok, and Barcelona.

Espionage Martini

3 fl oz citron vodka

$^1/_2$ fl oz crème de menthe (peppermint liqueur)

Method
Shake all ingredients with ice and strain into a chilled Martini glass. Garnish with a lemon twist.

Copper Martini

2 fl oz gin

1 fl oz triple sec

½ fl oz Campari

Method
Shake all ingredients with ice and strain into a chilled Martini glass. Garnish with a lemon twist.

Luxury Martini

2 fl oz gin

1 fl oz Pimm's No. 1

½ fl oz crème de banane (banana liqueur)

½ fl oz sweet vermouth

¼ fl oz lime cordial

4 dashes of Angostura bitters

James Pimm, the proprietor of an oyster bar in the City of London, invented the drink that bears his name in the 1840s. He offered his gin-based beverage, which also included quinine and a secret blend of herbs, as an aid to digestion. It was served in a small tankard known as a No. 1 cup. Apart from Pimm's No. 1, there have been five incarnations of Pimm's: No. 2 is based on whisky; No. 3 on brandy; No. 4 rum; No. 5 rye; and No. 6 vodka. Of these, Pimm's No. 1, No. 3, and No. 6 are still in production.

Method
Shake all ingredients with ice and strain into a chilled Martini glass. Garnish with a twist of lime.

Grappatini

2 fl oz grappa

1³/₄ fl oz sweet vermouth

¹/₄ fl oz maraschino syrup

2 dashes of Angostura bitters

Method
Shake all ingredients with ice and strain into a
chilled Martini glass. Garnish with a cherry.

Grappa, which is essentially Italian peasants'
firewater, is enjoying a bit of a glamorous
makeover these days. Traditionally, it is made
from the distillation of pomace, which is the
leftovers from the winemaking process (grape
skins, seeds, and stalks), but nowadays
producers are making single grape variety
versions, notably from Chardonnay, Pinot
Grigio, and Moscatel. These upmarket
grappas are often packaged in seriously over-
the-top bottles, sometimes containing
elaborate glass mini-sculptures and floating
pieces of gold leaf. For this drink, use grappa
de moscato (made from the aromatic
Moscatel grape variety) if you can find any.

Martini Thyme

2¹/₂ fl oz gin

1¹/₂ fl oz green Chartreuse

¹/₂ fl oz sugar syrup

1 handful of lemon thyme (stalks removed)

Method
Muddle thyme with vodka in a shaker. Pour in
the Chartreuse and sugar syrup, shake with
ice and strain into a chilled Martini glass.
Garnish with three green olives threaded onto
a sprig of thyme.

Met Manhattan

2 fl oz bourbon

1 fl oz Grand Marnier

3/4 fl fl oz Teichenne
(butterscotch schnapps)

1 dash of orange bitters

This one's from the Met Bar at the
Metropolitan Hotel in London, one of the best
bars in the city for downing Martinis and
watching celebrities behaving badly.

Method
Shake all ingredients with ice and strain into a
chilled Martini glass. Garnish with an orange twist.

Allen Martini

2 fl oz gin

1 fl oz maraschino liqueur
(cherry liqueur)

1 fl oz freshly squeezed lemon juice

Method
Shake all ingredients with ice and strain into a
chilled Martini glass. Garnish with a lemon twist.

Nightmare Martini

1 1/2 fl oz gin

1 fl oz cherry brandy

1 fl oz Dubonnet red

1 fl oz freshly squeezed orange juice

A "mara" or "mare" is a malignant female
wraith in Scandinavian folklore believed to
cause nightmares. These immaterial
creatures entered the victim's room either
through the keyhole or under the door and
"rode" on their chest causing frightful
dreams. In Norwegian and Danish the
words for nightmare are "mareritt" and
"mareridt," meaning "mareride." In
Swedish it is "mardrom," or "maredream."
Mara's were also in the habit of entangling
the sleeper's hair, resulting in a condition
known as "marelocks"—a great excuse for
your next bad hair day.

Method
Shake all ingredients with ice and strain
into a chilled Martini glass. Garnish with
a cherry.

Mistletoe Martini

2 fl oz vodka

$^1/_2$ fl oz Midori (melon liqueur)

1 splash of grenadine

In Norse mythology the god Baldur was killed by a weapon made from mistletoe. He came back to life, however, when his mother Frigga, the goddess of love, washed away the mistletoe's poison with her tears. She was so overjoyed at her son's remarkable recovery that she kissed anyone who passed underneath the mistletoe to show her happiness and gratitude. This is why we kiss beneath the mistletoe at Christmas time.

Method
Shake the vodka and melon liqueur with ice and strain into a chilled Martini glass. Splash in the grenadine and watch it sink to the bottom of the glass for a festive red and green effect.

Park Avenue Martini

3 fl oz gin

$^1/_2$ fl oz sweet vermouth

$^1/_2$ fl oz freshly pressed pineapple juice

Method
Shake all ingredients with ice and strain into a chilled Martini glass. Garnish with a thin slice of pineapple.

Liquid Lover

2 fl oz Zubrowka (bison grass vodka)

³/₄ fl oz Parfait Amour (rose petal, vanilla, and almond flavored liqueur)

³/₄ fl oz lime cordial

¹/₂ fl oz freshly squeezed lemon juice

¹/₂ fl oz chilled water

Method
Give the ingredients a thorough shaking with some ice then pour through a strainer into a chilled cocktail glass.

Rat Pack Manhattan

1¹/₂ fl oz bourbon

¹/₂ fl oz Grand Marnier

¹/₂ fl oz sweet vermouth

¹/₂ fl oz dry vermouth

4 dashes of Angostura bitters

Method
Swirl the Grand Marnier around a chilled Martini glass and discard. Shake the bourbon, vermouth and Angostura bitters with ice and strain into the glass. Garnish with a cherry.

The Rat Pack included many famous faces over the years, including Humphrey Bogart, Lauren Bacall, and David Niven, but the most celebrated line-up was Frank Sinatra, Dean Martin, and Sammy Davis Jr. Frequent performers in Las Vegas, they were instrumental in ending the segregation of audiences in its hotels and casinos, as they refused to play any venue that would not give full service to Sammy Davis. Angie Dickinson was often referred to as the Rat Pack Mascot and Shirley MacLaine was an honorary member, being the only woman to be considered "one of the boys."

Melrose Martini

2¹/₂ fl oz vodka

³/₄ fl oz triple sec

³/₄ fl oz cranberry juice

Method
Shake all ingredients with ice and strain into a chilled Martini glass. Garnish with an orange twist.

Veritas

1 fl oz gin

1 fl oz triple sec

1 fl oz freshly squeezed lime juice

$1/2$ fl oz crème de cassis
(blackcurrant liqueur)

Method
Shake the gin, triple sec, and lime juice with
ice and strain into a chilled Martini glass.
Carefully pour the cassis over the back of a
teaspoon over the surface of the drink.
Garnish with a lemon twist.

In vino veritas means that people usually tell
the truth when under the influence of alcohol,
though a polygraph or lie detector is usually
more reliable. Invented by John A Larson, it
measures blood pressure, heart rate, and
breathing while the subject answers tricky
questions. Polygraph testing is by no means
fool-proof, however. Aldrich Ames passed
two such tests while he was spying for the
Russian government. His Soviet handlers had
given him some invaluable advice on how to
beat the machine: just relax.

Old Fashioned Martini

3 fl oz vodka

$1/2$ fl oz bourbon

$1/2$ fl oz freshly squeezed orange juice

1 dash of Angostura bitters

1 dash of sugar syrup

Method
Shake all ingredients with ice and strain into a
chilled Martini glass. Garnish with a cherry.

Opal Martini

2 fl oz gin

1 fl oz triple sec

2 fl oz freshly squeezed orange juice

Method

Shake all ingredients with ice and strain into a
Martini glass. Garnish with a flamed orange twist.

Clover Club Martini

3 fl oz gin

1¹/₂ fl oz freshly squeezed lemon juice

¹/₂ fl oz grenadine

Method

Shake all ingredients with ice and strain into a
chilled Martini glass. Garnish with an orange
twist.

On a lucky four-leaf clover, according to
folklore, one leaf represents hope, another
faith, another love, and the fourth leaf signifies
luck. Unfortunately, there are roughly 10,000
three-leaf clovers for every four-leaf example.
An 18-leaf clover is recorded in the Guinness
Book of World Records. Now that's what I
call lucky.

Mrs Robinson Martini

3 fl oz vodka

$^1/_2$ fl oz limoncello (lemon liqueur)

$^1/_2$ fl oz freshly squeezed orange juice

Method
Shake all ingredients with ice and strain into a chilled Martini glass. Garnish with an orange twist.

Great Mughal Martini

20 raisins

$1^1/_2$ fl oz bourbon

$^1/_4$ fl oz sugar syrup

$^3/_4$ fl oz passion fruit syrup

$^1/_4$ fl oz freshly squeezed lime juice

1 fl oz lime cordial

3 drops of rose water

If you have the time and inclination you could infuse a bottle of bourbon with raisins rather than following the instructions below.

Method
Muddle the raisins with the bourbon in the base of a shaker. Pour in the sugar syrup, passion fruit syrup, lime juice, cordial, and rose water, shake with ice and strain into a chilled Martini glass. Garnish with a small piece of lemon grass for an authentic Indian flavor.

Katinka

2 fl oz vodka

$^1/_2$ fl oz apricot brandy

$^1/_2$ fl oz freshly squeezed lime juice

6 fresh mint leaves

Method
Muddle the mint leaves with the vodka in the base of a shaker. Pour in the apricot brandy and lime juice, shake with ice and strain into a chilled Martini glass. Garnish with a lime twist.

Cinnamon Limeade Martini

2 fl oz vodka

1 fl oz cinnamon schnapps

$^1/_2$ fl oz lime cordial

$^1/_2$ fl oz chilled water

Method
Shake all ingredients with ice and strain into a chilled Martini glass. Garnish with a twist of lime.

Piscotini

2 fl oz pisco (clear South American brandy)

$^1/_2$ fl oz absinthe

2 fl oz white grape juice

1 fl oz fresh pineapple juice

Method
Shake all ingredients with ice and strain into a chilled Martini glass. Garnish with a couple of white grapes on the stem draped over the rim of the glass. Very fancy.

Pisco is a white spirit distilled from grapes, which means it's a clear type of brandy. Both Chile and Peru claim it as their national spirit and the legal battle between the two countries is ongoing. In the Quecha language the birds that inhabit the valleys of the Ica region of Peru are called "pisco." One of the valleys was later named "Pisco" and the people who settled there during the Inca empire were called "Piskos." They made clay containers called "piscos" to store beverages. Oh, and Spanish sailors in the 17th century called the drink pisco after the port of Pisco where they used to buy it. So there you have it: "pisco" is the name of a drink, a bird, a port, a clay container, a valley, and a people.

Rendezvous Martini

3 fl oz gin

1 fl oz cherry brandy

$^1/_2$ fl oz Campari

Method
Shake all ingredients with ice and strain into a chilled Martini glass. Garnish with a cherry.

Polish Martini

1$^1/_2$ fl oz Cognac

1 fl oz Mandarine Napoleon

$^1/_2$ fl oz apricot brandy

1 fl oz freshly squeezed orange juice

$^1/_2$ a fresh egg white

4 dashes of Angostura bitters

The first model to appear as Playmate of the Month in *Playboy* magazine was Margie Harrison, Miss January 1954, in the second issue. Marilyn Monroe featured in the first issue as Sweetheart of the Month.

Method
Shake all ingredients with ice and strain into a chilled Martini glass. Garnish with an orange twist.

Q Martini

The James Bond Martini references just keep on coming. Q stands for Quartermaster and is the head of Q Branch, the fictional research and development division of the British Secret Service. Ian Fleming named the character after Geoffrey Boothroyd, a firearms expert who wrote to Fleming suggesting that Bond was not using the best weaponry. Some of his more memorable gadgets include the Aston Martin with ejector seat in *Goldfinger* and who could forget the ghetto-blaster rocket launcher in *The Living Daylights*.

3 fl oz vodka

$^1/_2$ fl oz blue curacao

Method
Shake all ingredients with ice and strain into a chilled Martini glass. Garnish with an orange twist.

Mary Pickford

2 fl oz white rum

2 fl oz freshly pressed pineapple juice

1 dash of grenadine

Method
Shake all ingredients with ice and strain into a chilled Martini glass. Garnish with a cherry.

Born plain, old Gladys Smith in Toronto in 1892, Mary Pickford became one of the first great female movie stars of the silent era. Films were made a good deal quicker in those early days, and in 1909 alone, at the height of her fame, Mary Pickford appeared in 51 films—that's nearly one a week. By the time she was 20 she'd been in 176 films. With her diminutive frame (she stood only 5-feet tall), her Panda-eye make-up and Cupid's bow lips, Mary Pickford was taken to heart by the American people who called her, quite simply, America's Sweetheart.

Red Neck Martini

2¹/₂ fl oz Scotch whisky

1 fl oz Dubonnet red

1 fl oz cherry brandy

Method
Shake all ingredients with ice and strain into a chilled Martini glass. Garnish with an orange twist.

Collection Martini

1½ fl oz citron vodka

¾ fl oz Benedictine

¾ fl oz crème de mure (blackberry liqueur)

½ fl oz freshly squeezed lime juice

Method
Shake all ingredients with ice and strain into a chilled Martini glass. Garnish with a lime twist.

Desperate Blackberry Martini

3 fl oz gin

½ fl oz dry vermouth

½ fl oz blackberry brandy

Method
Shake all ingredients with ice and strain into a chilled Martini glass. Garnish with a fresh blackberry.

Rum Martini

2½ fl oz white rum

1½ fl oz dry vermouth

Method
Shake the rum and dry vermouth with ice and strain into a chilled Martini glass. Garnish with a lemon twist or an olive.

El Floridita Martini

1½ fl oz vodka

1½ fl oz white rum

¾ fl oz lime juice

¾ fl oz sweet vermouth

½ fl oz white crème de cacao
(chocolate liqueur)

Method
Shake all ingredients with ice and strain into a
chilled Martini glass. Garnish with a lime twist.

There is a seat at the corner of the El Floridita
bar in Havana that is still reserved for Ernest
Hemingway. It was his favorite watering hole
in Cuba and the place where he would
entertain his friends, such as Spencer Tracy,
Errol Flynn, and Gary Cooper. He used to
enjoy watching the bartenders practicing their
craft and they created a cocktail called the
Papa Doble in his honor. It comprised 3 fl oz
of white rum, the juice of two limes, half a
grapefruit, and 6 drops of cherry brandy,
whisked in a blender.

Cameron Martini

2 fl oz Scotch whisky

1¼ fl oz amaretto (almond liqueur)

1¼ fl oz freshly squeezed lemon juice

½ fl oz chilled water (optional)

Method
Shake all ingredients with ice and strain into a
chilled Martini glass. Garnish with a lemon twist.

Southern Tea-Knee

1½ fl oz Southern Comfort

½ fl oz gin

½ fl oz crème de banane
(banana liqueur)

½ fl oz apricot brandy

1½ fl oz strong cold Earl Grey tea

Earl Grey is a black tea blend flavored with oil
extracted from the rind of the bergamot
orange. It is named after Charles Grey, 2nd
Earl Grey, who is said to have received some
as a diplomatic gift either from India or China.

Method
Shake all ingredients with ice and strain into a
chilled Martini glass. Garnish with an apricot slice.

Peggy Sue's Martini

2¹/₂ fl oz gin

¹/₂ fl oz sweet vermouth

¹/₂ fl oz Dubonnet

¹/₂ fl oz Pernod

Method
Shake all ingredients with ice and strain into a chilled Martini glass. Garnish with a lemon twist.

Peggy Sue by Buddy Holly and The Crickets reached number three on the Billboard Hot 100 in 1957. It was originally called *Cindy Lou* but was changed in honour of The Cricket's drummer Jerry Allison's girlfriend and, later, wife who played some of the drums on the record. Holly recorded a demo for a sequel called *Peggy Sue Got Married*, which remained undiscovered until after his untimely death.

Star Martini

2 fl oz gin

1 fl oz calvados

¹/₂ fl oz dry vermouth

¹/₂ fl oz sweet vermouth

¹/₂ fl oz freshly squeezed grapefruit juice

Method
Shake all ingredients with ice and strain into a chilled Martini glass. Garnish with a cherry.

Tuxedo Martini

2¹/₂ fl oz gin

1 fl oz dry vermouth

¹/₂ fl oz fino sherry

1 teaspoon absinthe

1 teaspoon maraschino liqueur (cherry liqueur)

3 dashes of orange bitters

Method
Shake all ingredients with ice and strain into a chilled Martini glass. Garnish with an orange twist.

Black tie is the dress code for formal evening events that are not formal enough to require a white tie. Up until 1865, white tie, worn with a tailcoat, was the only acceptable form of evening dress, but it was in this year that Henry Poole & Co of Savile Row in London made a "short smoking jacket" for the Prince of Wales. The Prince paired it with a black tie and the fashion soon spread among his circle.

Veneto

2 fl oz Cognac

¹/₄ fl oz white sambuca

¹/₄ fl oz freshly squeezed lemon juice

¹/₄ fl oz sugar syrup

¹/₂ a fresh egg white

Method
Shake all ingredients with ice and strain into a
chilled Martini glass. Garnish with a lemon twist.

Claridge

1¹/₂ fl oz gin

1¹/₂ fl oz dry vermouth

³/₄ fl oz apricot brandy

³/₄ fl oz triple sec

Method
Shake all ingredients with ice and strain into a
chilled Martini glass. Garnish with an orange twist.

The royal connections of Claridge's Hotel in
Mayfair, London, are such that it is sometimes
referred to as an "extension of Buckingham
Palace." Founded in 1812, the hotel's reputation
was sealed in 1860 when Empress Eugenie
of France made an extended visit there and
entertained Queen Victoria in her rooms.

Hasty Martini

3 fl oz gin

¹/₂ fl oz dry vermouth

4 dashes of Pernod

2 dashes of grenadine

Method
Shake all ingredients with ice and strain into a
chilled Martini glass. Garnish with a lemon
twist.

Mick Jagger-meister

1 fl oz vodka

1 fl oz Jägermeister (herbal liqueur)

$\frac{1}{2}$ fl oz freshly squeezed lemon juice

$\frac{1}{2}$ fl oz sugar syrup

Method
Shake all ingredients with ice and strain into a chilled Martini glass. Garnish with a lemon twist.

Jägermeister, which means "master hunter," is a herbal-flavored curiosity from Germany where it's often used as an aid to digestion and for settling upset stomachs. On its iconic label there's a stag's head with a cross floating between its antlers depicting the story of St Hubert. What do you mean, you don't know the story of St Hubert? He was hunting in the Ardennes in France when he saw a stag with a crucifix above its head. Imagine his surprise when the animal turned to him and said, "Hubert, unless thou turnest to the Lord and leadest an holy life, thou shalt quickly go down to hell." Hubert, by all accounts, turned to the Lord pretty quickly.

Wow

1 fl oz Cognac

1 fl oz Calvados

1 fl oz golden rum

Method
Shake all ingredients with ice and strain into a chilled Martini glass. Garnish with am orange twist.

Betweenytini

1 fl oz rum

1 fl oz Cognac

1 fl oz triple sec

1 teaspoon freshly squeezed lemon juice

$\frac{1}{2}$ fl oz sugar syrup (to taste)

Here's a Martini-sized version of the classic Between the Sheets cocktail. Invented in the 1930s, the golden era for classy concoctions, the BTS is a seductive nightcap comprising equal parts Cognac, rum, and triple sec with just a smidgen of lemon juice.

Method
Shake all ingredients with ice and strain into a Martini glass. Garnish with a flamed orange twist.

Waldorf Martini

2^1/$_2$ fl oz bourbon

1 fl oz Pernod

^{1}/$_2$ fl oz sweet vermouth

1 dash of Angostura bitters

Method
Shake all ingredients with ice and strain into a chilled Martini glass. Garnish with a lemon twist.

The Waldorf=Astoria is not one, but two luxury hotels in New York City. Note the important "equals sign;" it represents the connection, known as Peacock Alley, between the Waldorf Hotel, opened by William Waldorf Astor, and the Astoria Hotel, opened by his cousin, John Jacob Astor IV. The hotel(s) has its (their) own platform at the Grand Central Terminal.

savourytinis

Gilroy Martini

3 fl oz Zubrowka (bison grass vodka)

1 fl oz dry vermouth

2 drops of garlic juice

Method
Shake all ingredients with ice and strain into a chilled Martini glass. Garnish with a green olive.

Garlic (*Allium sativum*) is also known as the "stinking rose." While humans have grown to love its pungent qualities, the plant creates its trademark stink when it is damaged to dissuade birds, insects, and worms from eating it. Perhaps because of this, and because of its reputation as a powerful preventative medicine, garlic is also used to ward off devils, werewolves, and, of course, vampires.

Onion Ring Martini

2 rings of fresh red onion

2 fl oz gin

1 fl oz sake rice wine

4 dashes of orange bitters

$1/2$ teaspoon sugar syrup

Method
Muddle the onion with the gin in the base of a shaker, pour in the remaining ingredients, shake with ice and strain into a chilled Martini glass. Garnish with an onion ring.

Bloody Bull

$1^1/_2$ fl oz tequila

$1/_2$ fl oz freshly squeezed lemon juice

$1^1/_2$ fl oz tomato juice

$1^1/_2$ fl oz beef bouillon

4 drops of Worcestershire sauce

4 drops of Tabasco sauce

Method
Rim a chilled Martini glass with salt and pepper before starting to make the drink. Shake all ingredients with ice and strain into the glass.

181

Cajun Martini

2 fl oz vodka

1 fl oz dry vermouth

1 jalapeño pepper

The Cajuns are an ethnic group, descendants of Acadians, who were expelled from Nova Scotia by the British between 1755 and 1763. They are essentially French Canadians with the addition of local peoples such as the Abenaki and Mikmaq.

Method
Shake the vodka and vermouth with ice and strain into a Martini glass. Garnish with the jalapeño pepper.

Saltecca

3 fl oz tequila

$^3/_4$ fl oz dry fino Sherry

$^1/_4$ fl oz brine from a jar of capers

$^1/_4$ fl oz sugar syrup

$^1/_2$ fl oz chilled water

Method
Shake all ingredients with ice and strain into a chilled Martini glass. Garnish with a lemon twist.

Shrimptini

3 fl oz gin

1 fl oz dry vermouth

1 dash of Tabasco sauce

1 cooked shrimp

Method
Shake the gin, vermouth, and Tabasco with ice and strain into a chilled Martini glass. Garnish with the shrimp.

Red Earl Martini

2 slices of root ginger (thumb-nail size)

8 fresh raspberries

2½ fl oz vodka

¾ fl oz limoncello (lemon liqueur)

¼ fl oz sugar syrup

The Red Earl was created by Salvatore Calabrese at The Lanesborough in London for Charles Spencer, the late Princess Diana's brother.

Method
Muddle the ginger and raspberries with the vodka in the base of a shaker. Pour in the limoncello and sugar syrup. Shake with ice and strain into a chilled Martini glass. Garnish with a fresh raspberry.

Green Hornet

2 fl oz gin

1 fl oz dry vermouth

2 dashes of green Tabasco

Method
Shake all ingredients with ice and strain into a chilled Martini glass. Garnish with a green olive.

Tabasco hot pepper sauce, produced by the McIlhenny Company in Louisiana since 1868, has strong connections with the US military. During the Vietnam War, General S McIlhenny, who presided over McIlhenny Company and is the grandson of the company's founder, issued "The Charlie Ration Cookbook" which came wrapped around a 2-fl oz (60-gram) bottle of Tabasco sauce in a camouflaged, water-resistant container.

Hot & Dirty Martini

3 fl oz pepper vodka

$^1/_2$ fl oz dry vermouth

$^1/_4$ fl oz olive brine

Method
Shake all ingredients with ice and strain into a chilled Martini glass. Garnish with a jalapeño pepper.

Lemon & Spice Martini

$1^1/_2$ fl oz citron vodka

$1^1/_2$ fl oz chilli vodka

$^1/_2$ fl oz dry vermouth

Method
Shake all ingredients with ice and strain into a chilled Martini glass. Garnish with a lemon twist.

Strawberry & Balsamic Martini

4 fresh hulled strawberries

2 fl oz vodka

$^3/_4$ fl oz fraise (strawberry liqueur)

$^1/_4$ fl oz balsamic vinegar

Method
Muddle the strawberries with the vodka in the base of a shaker. Pour in the balsamic vinegar and fraise. Shake all ingredients with ice and strain into a chilled Martini glass. Garnish with a fresh strawberry.

Balsamic vinegar is a dark, sweet-tasting, viscous vinegar that has been made in Modena, Italy, since the Middle Ages. Its base ingredient is the juice of white grapes, typically of the Trebbiano variety. The finest (very expensive) versions are aged for up to 25 years and are made by transferring the liquid into a succession of different wooden casks to absorb the flavors of each type of wood: oak, mulberry, chestnut, cherry, juniper, and ash are the most commonly used.

Low Tide Martini

3 fl oz vodka

$^1/_2$ fl oz dry vermouth

1 teaspoon clam juice

1 smoked clam

Method
Shake the vodka, vermouth and clam juice with ice and strain into a chilled Martini glass. Plop in the smoked clam for garnish.

Moksha Martini

2 fl oz vodka

3 fresh basil leaves

2 slices of fresh ginger (thumb-nail size)

$^1/_2$ fl oz ginger syrup

$^1/_2$ fl oz apple liqueur

$^3/_4$ fl oz freshly squeezed lemon juice

In Hinduism, the concept of Moksha refers to liberation from the cycle of death and rebirth. It is seen as a transcendence of phenomenal being, of any sense of consciousness of time, space, and causation (karma). In fact, Moksha is viewed as analogous to Nirvana.

Method
Muddle the basil leaves and ginger with vodka in the base of a shaker. Pour in the ginger syrup, apple liqueur, and lemon juice, shake with ice and strain into a chilled Martini glass. Garnish with a basil leaf.

Rocky's Caesar Martini

2 fl oz pepper vodka

$2^1/_2$ fl oz Clamato

1 dash of Tabasco sauce

1 dash of Worcestershire sauce

1 pinch of fresh ground black pepper

The Bloody Caesar cocktail was created to celebrate the opening of Marco's Italian restaurant at the Calgary Inn in Canada in 1969.

Method
Shake all ingredients, except the black pepper, with ice and strain into a chilled Martini glass. Garnish with the black pepper and a lime twist.

Aquavit Clamtini

2 fl oz aquavit

2 fl oz Clamato

1 teaspoon freshly
squeezed lemon juice

1 dash of Worcestershire sauce

1 dash of Tabasco sauce

Aquavit, or akvavit, is a Scandinavian spirit
distilled from grain or potatoes and flavored
with caraway seed. Occasionally, it is flavored
with cumin, dill, fennel, or coriander. It is
usually drunk ice-cold by the shot with
herring, crayfish, or smoked fish.

Method
Shake all ingredients with ice and strain into a
chilled Martini glass. Garnish with a lemon twist.

Raging Bull

1½ fl oz vodka

3 fl oz tomato juice

1 dash of Worcestershire sauce

1 dash of Tabasco, salt and pepper

1 dash of freshly squeezed lemon juice

Method
Shake all ingredients with ice and strain into a
chilled Martini glass. Garnish with a thin stick
of celery.

Pepper Martini

2 fl oz pepper-infused vodka

1¹/₂ fl oz dry vermouth

1 fresh jalapeño pepper

To make the pepper-infused vodka: take 3 red or green jalapeño peppers and cut them in half lengthways. Push them into a bottle of vodka with 2 peeled cloves of garlic.

Method
Shake the vodka and vermouth with ice and strain into a chilled Martini glass. Garnish with a jalapeño pepper.

Salty Dog

2 fl oz vodka

2 fl oz freshly squeezed grapefruit juice

1 teaspoon freshly squeezed lemon juice

Salt

Method
Rim a chilled Martini glass with the lemon juice and salt. Pour in the vodka and grapefruit juice, shake with ice and strain into a chilled Martini glass.

Respect

1 fl oz bourbon

1¹/₂ fl oz Southern Comfort

Tabasco to taste

1 jumbo shrimp

Method
Shake the bourbon and Southern Comfort with ice and strain into a chilled Martini glass. Splash in as much, or as little, Tabasco as you can take. Garnish with the jumbo shrimp.

187

Creole Martini

2 fl oz rum

1¹/₂ fl oz beef bouillon

1 teaspoon freshly squeezed lemon juice

1 dash of Tabasco sauce

1 pinch of salt

1 pinch of black pepper

Method
Shake all ingredients with ice and strain into a chilled Martini glass. Garnish with a lemon twist.

Saltillo

1¹/₂ fl oz tequila

4 fl oz freshly squeezed grapefruit juice

1 pinch of salt

Method
Shake the vodka and grapefruit juice with ice and strain into a chilled Martini glass. Sprinkle a pinch of salt over the top and garnish with a lime twist.

Red Snapper

2 fl oz gin

2 fl oz tomato juice

¹/₄ fl oz sherry

¹/₂ fl oz freshly squeezed lemon juice

4 drops of Tabasco sauce

4 drops of Worcestershire sauce

1 pinch of celery salt

1 pinch of black pepper

Sir Charles Sandys, Chief Justice of India, returned to England from the subcontinent with a recipe for curry powder that his wife, Lady Sandys, passed on to a pharmacy in Worcester to be reproduced. The pharmacy, called Lea & Perrins, duly obliged and experimented with a liquid version to be used as a sauce.

Method
Rim a chilled Martini glass with celery salt and black pepper. Shake the remaining ingredients with ice and strain into a chilled Martini glass. Garnish with a cherry tomato on a stick.

Le Diamant

3 fl oz vodka

¹/₃ fl oz balsamic vinegar

Method
Shake all ingredients with ice and strain into a chilled Martini glass. Garnish with fresh tarragon.

Smoked Salmon Martini

3 fl oz vodka

$^1/_2$ fl oz dry vermouth

1 dash of freshly squeezed lemon juice

1 small piece smoked salmon

Smoked salmon is a delicacy originating in Scotland. Typically, it is made from a salmon fillet that has been cured with salt and sometimes sugar and then is hot or cold smoked.

Method
Shake the vodka, vermouth, and lemon juice with ice and strain into a chilled Martini glass. Garnish with a small roll of smoked salmon on a cocktail stick.

Basil Beauty

4 fresh basil leaves

$2^1/_2$ fl oz citron vodka

2 fl oz freshly pressed pineapple juice

1 whole passion fruit

$^1/_4$ fl oz freshly squeezed lime juice

$^1/_2$ fl oz coconut milk

Method
Muddle the basil leaves with the vodka in the base of a shaker. Scoop in the contents of the passion fruit. Pour in the pineapple, lime juice and coconut milk, shake with ice and strain into a chilled Martini glass. Garnish with a thin slice of pineapple.

189

winetinis

Sangria Martini

Method
Shake all ingredients with ice and strain into a chilled Martini glass. Garnish with an orange twist.

1 fl oz red wine

1³/₄ fl oz Cognac

¹/₂ fl oz apple schnapps

¹/₂ fl oz chambord (raspberry liqueur)

1 fl oz freshly squeezed orange juice

¹/₂ fl oz sugar syrup

Bubbly Martini

2 shots vodka

Champagne to top up

The correct way to open a bottle of Champagne is to tilt the bottle away from you at an angle of about 45 degrees, hold the cork still and gently twist the bottle. This should cause the least wastage as the cork leaves with a sigh rather than a seismic pop.

Method
Pour vodka into a Martini glass and top up with chilled Champagne. Garnish with a strawberry.

Floof

2 fl oz raspberry vodka

1 fl oz chambord (raspberry liqueur)

Chilled Champagne to top up

Method
Shake the vodka and chambord with ice and strain into a chilled Martini glass. Top up with chilled Champagne and garnish with a fresh raspberry.

Red Angel

2 fl oz red wine

1 fl oz Grand Marnier

¹/₄ fl oz maraschino liqueur (cherry liqueur)

1 fl oz chilled water

Method
Shake all ingredients with ice and strain into a chilled Martini glass. Garnish with a cherry.

Renaissance

3 fl oz gin

¹/₂ fl oz dry fino Sherry

1 pinch of nutmeg

Method
Shake all ingredients with ice and strain into a chilled Martini glass. Garnish with a pinch of grated nutmeg.

US Martini

1¹/₂ fl oz vanilla-infused Cognac

1¹/₄ fl oz Sauvignon Blanc wine

1¹/₂ fl oz freshly pressed pineapple juice

¹/₄ fl oz sugar syrup

Created by cocktail guru Simon Difford, the US Martini takes its name from the initials for Ugni Blanc, the principal grape variety of Cognac, and Sauvignon Blanc, the main white grape variety of Bordeaux.

Method
Shake all ingredients with ice and strain into a chilled Martini glass. Garnish with a vanilla pod.

Nome

1½ fl oz gin

1½ fl oz dry fino Sherry

1 fl oz Yellow Chartreuse

Method
Shake all ingredients with ice and strain into a chilled Martini glass. Garnish with a lemon twist.

Fino Martini

3 fl oz gin

½ fl oz dry fino Sherry

Method
Shake all ingredients with ice and strain into a chilled Martini glass. Garnish with a lemon twist.

Having long been the top tipple of grandmothers and elderly aunts, Sherry is enjoying something of a fashionable revival; especially the straw-colored, dry fino style, which should be drunk fresh and chilled from the cooler. Its bone-dry, slightly salty tang works surprisingly well with sushi and adds levels of complexity to numerous cocktails. For sweeter styles, try the unctuously rich Pedro Ximenez or Cream Sherries.

Martini Royale

1½ fl oz vodka

½ fl oz crème de cassis (blackcurrant liqueur)

Champagne to top up

Method
Shake the vodka and crème de cassis with ice and strain into a chilled Martini glass. Top up with chilled Champagne and garnish with a blackberry.

With the simple addition of vodka, this is a Martini-style rendition of a French classic. Allegedly, the Mayor of Dijon and hero of the French resistance, Canon Felix Kir (1876-1968) popularized a splash of cassis in the local Bourgogne Aligote wine to render it more palatable during wartime. When Champagne is used the drink is elevated from the humble Kir to a Kir Royale.

Vanitini

2 fl oz vanilla vodka

2 fl oz Sauvignon Blanc wine

$\frac{1}{2}$ fl oz pineapple liqueur

$\frac{1}{4}$ fl oz crème de mure
(blackberry liqueur)

Method
Shake all ingredients with ice and strain into a chilled Martini glass. Garnish with a thin slice of pineapple.

In the Sack

2 fl oz cream Sherry

2 fl oz freshly squeezed orange juice

1 fl oz apricot nectar

$\frac{1}{2}$ fl oz freshly squeezed lemon juice

"In the Sack," get it? Sack is an old English word for Sherry, deriving from the French word "sec," meaning dry. Shakespeare's lovable rogue, Sir John Falstaff orders sack by the quart in *The Merry Wives of Windsor*. In *Henry IV, Part I* he says to Prince Hal, "If sack and sugar be a fault, God help the wicked!" It didn't help him.

Method
Shake all ingredients with ice and strain into a chilled Martini glass. Garnish with an orange twist.

Japanese Pear Martini

2 fl oz vodka

1 fl oz sake rice wine

$\frac{1}{2}$ fl oz Poire William liqueur
(pear flavored eau de vie)

Method
Shake all ingredients with ice and strain into a chilled Martini glass. Garnish with a slice of pear on the rim of the glass.

Flirtini

1 fl oz vodka

³/₄ fl oz triple sec

2 fl oz freshly pressed pineapple juice

Chilled Champagne to top up

Method
Shake the vodka, triple sec and pineapple juice with ice and strain into a chilled Martini glass. Top up with chilled Champagne and garnish with a cherry.

Here are some top tips for successful flirting from Peta Heskell who runs the Attraction Academy. For women: "Get lost, nerd" is not the way to say no; and carry something (a "flirting prop") to get you noticed is a good idea. For men: make sure your hair is clean and your body and breath smell good; and don't do the rounds of a group of women as this will make you look like a loser and the women may think you're desperate. For both sexes: be interesting by being interested.

Sake-politan

3 fl oz sake rice wine

³/₄ fl oz triple sec

³/₄ fl oz cranberry juice

¹/₄ fl oz freshly squeezed lime juice

Method
Shake all ingredients with ice and strain into a chilled Martini glass. Garnish with an orange twist.

East Indian

2 fl oz dry fino Sherry

2 fl oz dry vermouth

2 dashes of orange bitters

Method
Shake all ingredients with ice and strain into a chilled Martini glass. Garnish with an orange twist.

Red Dog Martini

3 fl oz vodka

½ fl oz ruby Port

2 teaspoons freshly squeezed lime juice

1 teaspoon grenadine

Port, from the majestic Douro Valley in Portugal, is red wine fortified by the addition of roughly one-fifth brandy. The classification of Port is extremely confusing, but there are essentially two main styles, wood-aged and bottle-aged. The former, not surprisingly, are aged in wooden barrels and are ready to drink as soon as they are bottled. These include Tawny, Colheita, LBV, Vintage Character, and Ruby Port, the last of which is designed to be drunk young, fruity, and fiery. Bottle-aged Ports start their lives in barrels but might then be aged in bottles, unfiltered, for 20 to 30 years.

Method

Shake all ingredients with ice and strain into a chilled Martini glass. Garnish with a lime twist.

Raspberry Saketini

2 fl oz raspberry vodka

1¼ fl oz sake rice wine

½ fl oz crème de cassis (blackcurrant liqueur)

1½ fl oz fresh pineapple juice

Method

Shake all ingredients with ice and strain into a Martini glass. Garnish with a couple of floating raspberries.

Vante Martini

4 pods of cardamom

1½ fl oz vanilla vodka

1½ fl oz Sauvignon Blanc wine

1 fl oz Licor 43 (Cuarenta Y Tres) liqueur

½ fl oz freshly pressed pineapple juice

Licor 43 is so named because it contains 43 ingredients, mostly fruits and herbs from the Mediterranean.

Method

Muddle the cardamom pods in the base of a shaker. Pour in the vodka, wine, liqueur, and pineapple juice, shake with ice and strain into a chilled Martini glass. Garnish with an orange twist.

Pappy Honeysuckle

2 fl oz Irish whiskey

2 teaspoons runny honey

1¼ fl oz Sauvignon Blanc wine

1½ fl oz freshly pressed apple juice

½ fl oz passion fruit syrup

¼ fl oz freshly squeezed lemon juice

The Sauvignon Blanc grape variety is the signature white grape from Bordeaux and is responsible for some of the world's greatest white wines, including Sancerre and Pouilly-Fume from the Loire. More recently, the New Zealanders have adopted Sauvignon Blanc as their own to produce such cult classics as Cloudy Bay. Popular tasting notes for wines made from Sauvignon Blanc include "herbaceous," "grassy," "nettles," and "cat's pee on a gooseberry bush," which, believe it or not, is meant to be complimentary.

Method
Stir the honey into the whiskey in the base of a shaker. Pour in the wine, apple juice, passion fruit syrup and lemon juice, shake with ice and strain into a chilled Martini glass. Garnish with a physalis fruit.

Crazy Fin

2 fl oz vodka

1 fl oz dry fino Sherry

1 fl oz triple sec

¼ fl oz freshly squeezed lemon juice

Method
Shake all ingredients with ice and strain into a chilled Martini glass. Garnish with a lemon twist.

The Ritz Cocktail

1½ fl oz Cognac

½ fl oz triple sec

¼ fl oz freshly squeezed lemon juice

¼ fl oz maraschino liqueur (cherry liqueur)

Chilled Champagne to top up

"Now if you're blue and don't know where to go to, why don't you go where fashion sits, Puttin' on the Ritz. Different types who wear a daycoat, pants with stripes and cutaway coat, perfect fits, Puttin' on the Ritz" – Irving Berlin (1929).

Method
Shake the Cognac, triple sec, maraschino liqueur, and lemon juice with ice and strain into a chilled Martini glass. Top up with chilled Champagne and garnish with a cherry.

197

Milano Martini

3 fl oz gin

³/₄ fl oz dry vermouth

³/₄ fl oz dry white wine

¹/₄ fl oz Campari

Method
Shake all ingredients with ice and strain into a chilled Martini glass. Garnish with an orange twist.

Sake-tini

1¹/₂ fl oz gin

2¹/₂ fl oz sake rice wine

¹/₂ fl oz Grand Marnier

Method
Shake all ingredients with ice and strain into a chilled Martini glass. Garnish with a lemon twist.

In Japan, where sake rice wine originates, "sake" simply means alcoholic drink. It is thought to date back to the third century with the advent of wet rice cultivation. The first sake was called "kuchikami no sake," or "chewing-in-the-mouth sake" because it was made by an entire village chewing rice, chestnuts, millet, acorn, and spitting the mixture into a tub. The enzymes from the saliva allowed the starches to saccharify (convert to sugar) and produce alcohol. Thankfully, the sake in your hand will not have been made this way.

Alaska Martini

2¹/₂ fl oz gin

1 fl oz dry fino Sherry

³/₄ fl oz Yellow Chartreuse

2 dashes of orange bitters

Method
Shake all ingredients with ice and strain into a chilled Martini glass. Garnish with an orange twist.

The United States bought Alaska from Russia for US$7.2 million in 1867, which works out at about 2 cents per acre. This is what you might call a profit deal. With 591,000 square miles, Alaska is the largest State in the Union, being more than twice the size of Texas, the next biggest.

Sex & The City Flirtini

2 fl oz vodka

1 fl oz chambord (raspberry liqueur)

1 fl oz fresh pineapple juice

Chilled Champagne to top up

Method
Shake the vodka, chambord, and pineapple juice with ice and strain into a chilled Martini glass. Top up with Champagne and garnish with a pineapple slice and a cherry.

Twinkle

3 fl oz vodka

1 fl oz elderflower cordial

Prosecco to top up

Prosecco is the name of a white grape variety grown in the Conegliano and Valdobbiadene wine-growing regions to the north of Venice. The classic Bellini cocktail (sparkling wine with peach purée) was created in Harry's Bar in Venice, which is why this drink should always be made with Prosecco. Don't ever let any one fob you off with Champagne.

Method
Shake the vodka and elderflower cordial with ice and strain into a chilled Martini glass. Top up with chilled Prosecco and garnish with a lemon twist.

Diablo

2¹/₂ shots white Port

1 shot sweet red vermouth

1 dash of freshly squeezed lemon juice

Method
Shake all ingredients with ice and strain into a Martini glass. The Devil's Cocktail is a similarly demonic drink, using red Port and dry vermouth instead.

CC Bellini

3 fl oz Champagne

1 fl oz vodka

1 fl oz chambord (raspberry liqueur)

Method
Pour the chilled Champagne into an equally chilled Martini glass. Pour the vodka and chambord into a shaker and shake with ice. Pour it over the Champagne in the glass and garnish with a fresh raspberry.

California Martini

3 fl oz vodka

$\frac{1}{2}$ fl oz red wine

$\frac{1}{2}$ tablespoon dark rum

3 to 5 dashes of orange bitters

Method
Shake all ingredients with ice and strain into a chilled Martini glass. Garnish with an orange twist.

Wonder Martini

1 fl oz gin

1 fl oz claret (red Bordeaux wine)

$\frac{1}{2}$ fl oz sugar syrup

$\frac{1}{2}$ fl oz freshly squeezed lemon juice

Bordeaux wine is traditionally known as claret in England from the French word "clairet" meaning clear.

Method
Shake all ingredients with ice and strain into a chilled Martini glass. Garnish with a strawberry.

200

mocktinis

Noosa Sunset

1/2 fresh peach (stoned)

3 fl oz freshly pressed pineapple juice

1 teaspoon grenadine

Method
Blend the peach and pineapple juice with cracked ice in a sturdy blender and strain into a chilled Martini glass. Pour the teaspoon of grenadine over the top and garnish with a slice of peach.

Noosa is the name of a cluster of suburbs on the Sunshine Coast in South East Queensland, Australia. The Noosa area was originally home to numerous Aboriginal tribes including the Undumbi, the Dulingbara, and the Gabbi Gabbi. Noothera, the aboriginal name for the area, means "a place of shade." Perhaps they were referring to the little paper umbrellas used to decorate the local cocktails. Perhaps not.

Mocktini

3 fl oz tonic water

1 fl oz freshly squeezed lime juice

1/4 fl oz freshly squeezed lemon juice

Method
Stir all ingredients with ice and strain into a chilled Martini glass. Garnish with a green olive on a cocktail stick, just like a real Martini.

Boo Boo's Special Martini

2 fl oz fresh pineapple juice

2 fl oz freshly squeezed orange juice

$^1/_2$ fl oz freshly squeezed lemon juice

1 dash of grenadine

1 dash of Angostura bitters

The voice of Boo Boo Bear, Yogi's little friend, was provided by the late Don Messick. But did you know he was also the voice of Scooby-Doo throughout the 1970s and his little sidekick, Scrappy-Doo, throughout the 1980s? What's more, he was also the voice of lugubrious mutt Droopy.

Method
Shake all ingredients with ice and strain into a Martini glass. Garnish with a slice of pineapple and a maraschino cherry.

PMS

2 fl oz freshly squeezed orange juice

2 fl oz cranberry juice

Soda water to top up

Method
Shake all ingredients with ice and strain into a chilled Martini glass. Garnish with a lemon twist.

203

Witch's Kiss

4 fl oz tropical fruit juice

$1/2$ fl oz grenadine

1 dash of lemon juice

1 dash of sugar syrup

Soda water to top up

Method
Shake the tropical fruit juice, lemon juice, grenadine, and sugar syrup with ice and pour into a chilled Martini glass. Top up with chilled soda water and garnish with a lemon twist.

Nineteen people, six of them men, were executed after the notorious Salem witch trials in Massachusetts in 1692. It is widely thought that many of the accused simply fell foul of local jealousies and were persecuted for ulterior motives. However, in 1976, a psychologist called Linnda Caporeal discovered that the symptoms of the accused (convulsions, delirium, and hallucinations) matched those of ergot poisoning. Ergot is a poisonous fungus that grows on cereal grains, especially rye and wheat, which were widely grown in the Salem area.

Doctor's Orders

3 fl oz freshly squeezed grapefruit juice

$1/2$ fl oz freshly squeezed lime juice

$1/2$ fl oz sugar syrup

Tonic water to top up

Method
Shake all ingredients with ice and strain into a chilled Martini glass. Garnish with a lime twist.

Beach Blanket Bingo

$1 1/2$ fl oz cranberry juice

$1 1/2$ fl oz freshly squeezed grapefruit juice

$1 1/2$ fl oz soda water

Method
Shake the cranberry and grapefruit juice with ice and strain into a chilled Martini glass. Top up with soda water and garnish with a lemon twist.

Pink Champagne

3 fl oz freshly pressed
pink grapefruit juice

1/2 fl oz freshly squeezed lemon juice

1/2 fl oz freshly squeezed lime juice

1 fl oz sugar syrup

1 dash of grenadine

1 dash of Angostura bitters

Method
Shake all ingredients with ice and strain into a
chilled Martini glass. Garnish with a lemon twist.

Pussyfoot

1 1/2 fl oz freshly squeezed orange juice

1 1/2 fl oz freshly squeezed lemon juice

1 1/2 fl oz freshly squeezed lime juice

Soda water to top up

Method
Shake all ingredients with ice and strain into a
chilled Martini glass. Garnish with a lemon twist.

Ginger Mick

2 fl oz freshly pressed apple juice

1 fl oz freshly squeezed lemon juice

1/2 fl oz freshly squeezed lime juice

Chilled ginger ale to top up

Method
Shake all ingredients except the ginger ale
with ice and strain into a Martini glass. Top up
with ginger ale and garnish with a slice of apple.

Acapulco Gold

2 fl oz freshly pressed pineapple juice

1 fl oz freshly squeezed grapefruit juice

1 fl oz coconut milk

1 fl oz fresh cream

Acapulco's official name is Acapulco de Juárez. It is a city and major sea port on the Pacific coast of Mexico.

Method
Shake all ingredients with ice and strain into a chilled Martini glass. Garnish with a thin slice of pineapple.

Jersey Lily

4 fl oz chilled fizzy apple juice

2 dashes of Angostura bitters

1 dash of sugar syrup

Method
Pour the fizzy apple juice into a chilled Martini glass. Splash in the Angostura bitters and sugar syrup and garnish with a thin slice of apple floating on the surface.

In China, the bulbs of certain lily species, especially *Lilium brownii*, are eaten as root vegetables. They are most commonly sold in dry form and are traditionally eaten during the summer because of their alleged ability to reduce the body's internal heat. Sometimes they are stir-fried and used to thicken soups because of their potato-like starch content. Don't try this at home—at least not without a qualified horticulturist.

Mock Champagnetini

2 fl oz freshly squeezed grapefruit juice

1 fl oz freshly squeezed orange juice

1 dash of grenadine

Dry ginger ale to top up

Method
Shake all ingredients except the ginger ale with ice and strain into a Martini glass. Top up with ginger ale and garnish with an orange twist.

Lethal Weapon

4 fl oz vegetable juice
1 teaspoon chilli sauce
$1/2$ fl oz freshly squeezed lemon juice
1 pinch of salt
1 pinch of pepper

Method
Shake all ingredients with ice and strain into a
Martini glass. Garnish with a thin strip of celery.

Magic Island

2 fl oz freshly pressed apple juice
1 fl oz freshly squeezed grapefruit juice
1 fl oz coconut milk
$1/2$ fl oz double cream
1 dash of grenadine

Method
Shake the apple and grapefruit juice, coconut
milk, and double cream with ice and strain
into a chilled Martini glass. Splash in the
grenadine over the top and garnish with an
orange twist.

Greciantini

3 fl oz freshly squeezed peach juice
$1^1/2$ fl oz freshly squeezed orange juice
$3/4$ fl oz freshly squeezed lemon juice

Method
Shake all ingredients with ice and strain into a
chilled Martini glass. Garnish with a thin slice
of peach.

Mock White Sangriatini

4 fl oz white grape juice

1 fl oz freshly squeezed pink grapefruit juice

quarter fl oz freshly squeezed lime juice

Soda water to top up

Method
Shake the grape, grapefruit and lime juice
with ice and strain into a chilled Martini glass.
Top up with soda water and garnish with a
couple of white grapes.

Shirley Temple

Born in Santa Monica, California, in 1928, Shirley
Temple (her real name) started out in movies at
the age of three. Her golden curls and dimples
helped to bring some cheer to America after the
Great Depression, to the extent that she was the
box-office champion for three consecutive years
in 1936/37/38. Her contemporaries, Clarke Gable,
Bing Crosby, Gary Cooper, and Joan Crawford,
were probably less cheered by her runaway
success. In her adult years, Temple served as
an ambassador to Ghana and Czechoslovakia.

4 fl oz dry ginger ale

$^1/_4$ fl oz grenadine

Method
Pour the grenadine into a chilled Martini glass
and top up with chilled dry ginger ale. Garnish
with a lemon twist.

Caribbean Cocktail

$^1/_4$ of a fresh mango (peeled)

$^1/_4$ of a banana

Juice of half an orange

1 dash of freshly squeezed lime juice

Method
Blend the ingredients with some cracked ice
in a sturdy blender, strain into a chilled Martini
glass. Garnish with a slice of mango.

Montego Bay

3 fl oz freshly squeezed orange juice

$^1/_2$ fl oz freshly squeezed lemon juice

$^1/_2$ fl oz sugar syrup

1 dash of grenadine

Lemonade to top up

Famous for more romantic products like rum and coffee, Montego Bay in Jamaica actually takes its name from "manteca," which is the Spanish word for lard. It was from here, during the Spanish colonization of the island from 1511 to 1655, that Spanish ships were loaded up with lard, leather, and beef.

Method
Shake the orange and lemon juice, sugar syrup, and grenadine with ice and strain into a chilled Martini glass. Top up with lemonade and garnish with an orange twist.

Down East Delight

1 fl oz cranberry juice

1 fl oz freshly pressed pineapple juice

1 fl oz freshly squeezed orange juice

1 fl oz sugar syrup

Method
Shake all ingredients with ice and strain into a chilled Martini glass. Garnish with a lemon twist.

Cardinal Punch

2 fl oz cranberry juice

1 fl oz freshly squeezed orange juice

$^1/_2$ fl oz freshly squeezed lemon juice

Ginger ale to top up

Method
Shake cranberry, orange and lemon juice with ice and strain into a chilled Martini glass. Top up with chilled ginger ale and garnish with an orange twist.

Temperance Mocktail

Juice of 1 lemon

1 egg yolk

2 dashes of grenadine

Method
Shake all ingredients with ice and strain into a chilled Martini glass. Garnish with a cherry.

While the American period of Prohibition (1920-1933) remains one of the most far-reaching and extreme expressions of temperance, there have been temperance movements all around the world. In Australia in the late 1800s the sale of alcoholic drinks was banned after 6 pm. Somewhat predictably, this led to the rise of the "six o'clock swill" on the way home from work.

Mock Margarita

2 fl oz freshly squeezed lime juice

¹/₂ fl oz freshly squeezed lemon juice

¹/₂ fl oz freshly squeezed orange juice

1 fl oz sugar syrup

Method
Shake all ingredients with ice and strain into a chilled Martini glass. Garnish with a lime twist.

Danny Herrera, bartender at the Rancho La Gloria in Tijuana, Mexico, is generally credited with creating the very first Margarita cocktail in 1938. It is said that he came up with it for the benefit of the actress Marjorie King, who was allergic to all liquor with the notable exception of tequila (with many people it's usually the other way around). The Spanish version of Marjorie is Margarita, which, incidentally, means "daisy."

Sun Downer

4 fl oz white grape juice

2 fl oz sparkling water

1 fresh sprig of mint

Method
Stir the apple juice and sparkling water with ice and pour into a chilled Martini glass. Garnish with the fresh mint.

Jimmy's Beach Cruiser

2 fl oz raspberry juice

2 fl oz freshly squeezed orange juice

1/2 fl oz freshly pressed pineapple juice

Lemonade to top up

Method
Shake all ingredients with ice and strain into a chilled Martini glass. Garnish with a fresh raspberry.

Pac-Man

2 fl oz dry ginger ale

1 fl oz freshly squeezed lemon juice

1 fl oz sugar syrup

1 dash of grenadine

1 dash of Angostura bitters

Method
Shake all ingredients with ice and strain into a chilled Martini glass. Garnish with a small piece of stem ginger.

Pac-Man, or Pakkuman, the iconic arcade, game was launched by Namco in 1980. Invented by Toru Iwatani, the central figure in this game about eating was inspired by a pizza with one slice missing. "Pakupaku" is Japanese for "he eats, he eats." The first perfect Pac-Man score (3,333,360 points) was notched up by Billy Mitchell in the US, who completed all 255 levels without being caught by any of the ghosts. Their names, incidentally, are Inky, Pinky, Blinky, and Clyde.

Pearls & Lace

1 fl oz orange soda

1 fl oz Coca-Cola

1 fl oz root beer

1 fl oz lemon & lime soda

1 fl oz lemonade

Method
Pour all ingredients into a shaker with ice, stir gently and pour into a chilled Martini glass. Garnish with an orange twist.

Root beer is a fermented drink made from vanilla, cherry tree bark, licorice root, sarsaparilla root, sassafras root bark, nutmeg, anise, and molasses. Like real beer, it has a thick and foamy head when poured. Root beer was originally used as a medicine to treat coughs and mouth sores and the first commercially available, carbonated version was launched by Charles Elmer Hires in 1893. It also happens to be the favorite drink of Snoopy, Charles Schulz's cartoon beagle.

Nicholas

1¹/₂ fl oz freshly
squeezed grapefruit juice

1¹/₂ fl oz freshly squeezed orange juice

¹/₂ fl oz freshly squeezed lemon juice

¹/₂ fl oz sugar syrup

1 dash of grenadine

Method
Shake all ingredients with ice and strain into a
chilled Martini glass. Garnish with an orange twist.

San Francisco

1 fl oz freshly pressed pineapple juice

1 fl oz freshly squeezed orange juice

1 fl oz freshly squeezed grapefruit juice

¹/₂ fl oz freshly squeezed lemon juice

¹/₂ fl oz sugar syrup

2 dashes of grenadine

Soda water to top up

Method
Shake the pineapple, orange, grapefruit and
lemon juice, sugar syrup, and grenadine with
ice and strain into a chilled Martini glass. Top
up with soda water and garnish with a small
piece of pineapple.

Pina Colada Perfecto

3 fl oz fresh pineapple juice

1¹/₂ fl oz coconut milk

Method
Shake all ingredients with ice and strain into a
chilled Martini glass. Garnish with a slice of
pineapple.

Prairie Oyster

1 dash of virgin olive oil

1 egg yolk (unbroken)

1 or 2 tablespoons tomato ketchup

1 pinch of salt

1 pinch of freshly ground black pepper

1 dash of Worcestershire sauce

1 dash of white wine vinegar

Method
Rinse the glass with olive oil then pour it away. Add the tomato ketchup and plop in the egg yolk (unbroken). Season with the Worcestershire sauce, vinegar, salt, and pepper. Down it in one. You might want to serve this with a glass of iced water on the side.

No Martini book would be complete without a recipe for a hangover "cure." Of course, nothing but time can relieve the terrible feelings associated with excessive alcohol consumption, but the Prairie Oyster is thought to help.

Pony's Neck

4 fl oz dry ginger ale

$^1/_2$ fl oz freshly squeezed lime juice

2 dashes of Angostura bitters

Method
Shake all ingredients with ice and strain into a chilled Martini glass. Garnish with a lemon twist.

Princess Margaret

6 fresh strawberries

1 slice of fresh pineapple

Juice of half an orange

Juice of half a lemon

$^1/_2$ fl oz sugar syrup

The Princess Margaret, Countess of Snowdon, was the youngest daughter of King George VI of England and Queen Elizabeth. She was also the sister of Queen Elizabeth II. Despite being born into great privilege, Margaret suffered unrequited love, alleviated to some extent by wild partying at her holiday home on the island of Mustique. She fell in love with Group Captain Peter Woolridge Townsend, a Royal Air Force pilot who, unfortunately, was a divorcee and therefore considered to be unsuitable. After considerable inner conflict, and on the advice of the Archbishop of Canterbury, Margaret renounced Townsend amid suggestions that she might lose her title and her place in the line of succession.

Method
Blitz the strawberries and pineapple in a blender and transfer it to a shaker. Pour in the orange and lemon juice and sugar syrup, stir with ice and strain into a chilled Martini glass. Garnish with a fresh strawberry.

Rosy Pippin

4 fl oz freshly pressed apple juice

1 teaspoon lemon juice

1 dash of grenadine

Dry ginger ale to top up

Method
Shake all ingredients except ginger ale with ice and strain into a chilled Martini glass. Top up with ginger ale and garnish with a cherry.

Safer Sex on the Beach

2 fl oz cranberry juice

2 fl oz freshly squeezed grapefruit juice

1 fl oz peach nectar

Method
Shake all ingredients with ice and strain into a chilled Martini glass. Garnish with a cherry.

Nursery Fizz

2 fl oz freshly squeezed orange juice

2 fl oz ginger ale

Method
Stir ingredients with ice and strain into a chilled Martini glass. Garnish with a cherry.

Mock Caesartini

4 fl oz clamato juice (a blend of tomato juice and liquified clams)

$^1/_2$ fl oz freshly squeezed lemon juice

$^1/_2$ fl oz freshly squeezed lime juice

1 dash of Worcestershire sauce

1 dash of Tabasco sauce

Method
Shake all ingredients with ice and strain into a chilled Martini glass. Garnish with a thin stick of celery.

Snowball Special

3 fl oz cranberry juice

1$^1/_2$ fl oz freshly pressed apple juice

$^1/_2$ fl oz freshly squeezed orange juice

1 pinch of powdered cinnamon

Method
Shake the cranberry, apple, and orange juice with ice and strain into a chilled Martini glass. Garnish with a pinch of powdered cinnamon and an orange twist.

Shrinking Violet

3 fl oz red grape juice

$^1/_2$ fl oz lime juice

Chilled lemonade to top up

There's something about little girls called Violet. The catchphrase of Violet Elizabeth Bott, the arch enemy of William and his gang in Richmal Crompton's *Just William* books, was, "I'll thcream and thcream 'till I'm thick—I can, you know." Roald Dahl also used the name for his grizzly, gum-chewing creation, Violet Beauregarde, in *Charlie and the Chocolate Factory*. Ignoring grown-up advice against chewing a stick of experimental gum she went right ahead and did it—and was transformed into a child-sized blueberry. I'm sure there's a moral there somewhere.

Method
Shake the grape and lime juice with ice and strain into a chilled Martini glass. Top up with lemonade. You can garnish with a couple of red grapes.

I'll Fake Manhattan

2 fl oz freshly squeezed orange juice

2 fl oz cranberry juice

2 dashes of orange bitters

1 dash of grenadine

1 dash of freshly squeezed lemon juice

Manhattan is one of the smallest counties in the United States, but it is also the most densely populated in the country.

Method
Shake all ingredients with ice and strain into a chilled Martini glass. Garnish with a lemon twist.

Sunburnt Kiwi

3 fl oz red grape juice

$^1/_2$ fl oz freshly squeezed lemon juice

1 ripe plum (stoned)

1 kiwi fruit (skinned)

Kiwis, the national symbol of New Zealand, are any of the species of small, flightless birds (ratites) of the genus *apteryx* indigenous to that country. Kiwis are nocturnal creatures, but not wild party-goers. Far from it, they live as monogamous couples, often for as long as 20 years. Which is nice. But what's the point of a flightless bird anyway?

Method
Muddle the plum and kiwi fruit in the base of a shaker. Pour in the grape and lemon juice, shake with ice and strain into a Martini glass. Garnish with a slice of kiwi fruit.

Rosie's Special Mocktini

2 fl oz cold Earl Grey tea

2 fl oz freshly squeezed orange juice

Soda water to top up

Method
Rim a chilled Martini glass with sugar. Shake the cold tea and orange juice with ice and strain into the glass. Garnish with an orange twist.

Unfuzzy Naveltini

3 fl oz freshly squeezed orange juice

1½ fl oz freshly squeezed peach juice

1 dash of grenadine

Lemonade to top up

Method
Shake the orange and peach juice and grenadine with ice and pour into a chilled Martini glass. Top up with lemonade and garnish with a thin slice of peach.

Surfer's Paradise

4 fl oz lemonade

1 fl oz freshly squeezed lime juice

3 dashes of Angostura bitters

Was ever a better "car chase" committed to celluloid than in the closing scenes of *Mad Max 2, The Road Warrior*? Throughout this post-apocalyptic movie the terrorized good guys are dreaming of finding a place called Paradise. Apparently, the place about which they're fantasizing is none other than the real-life Surfer's Paradise on Australia's Gold Coast in Queensland.

Method
Stir all ingredients with ice in a shaker and pour into a chilled Martini glass. Garnish with a lemon twist.

Get Lucky

3 fl oz chocolate milk

1½ fl oz double cream

5 drops of peppermint cordial

Method
Shake all ingredients with ice and strain into a chilled Martini glass. Garnish with a sprig of fresh mint.

Rabbits' feet are considered lucky in many cultures but not on the Isle of Portland on the coast of Dorset in England. Men who were excavating the famous Portland limestone would often report seeing rabbits emerging from their burrows minutes before fatal landslides. To this day, one doesn't mention the "r" word in Portland where locals refer to the little varmints as "underground mutton" instead.

Tomato Cooltini

4 fl oz chilled tomato juice

½ fl oz freshly squeezed lemon juice

Soda water to top up

Method
Rim a chilled Martini glass with coarse salt. Shake tomato and lemon juice with ice and strain into the glass. Top up with tonic water and garnish with a thin strip of celery.

Transfusion

2 fl oz white grape juice

2 fl oz lemon & lime soda

$^1/_2$ fl oz freshly squeezed lime juice

Method
Stir all ingredients with ice in a shaker and strain into a chilled Martini glass. Garnish with a couple of white grapes.

Sunset Cool-tini

3 fl oz cranberry juice

2 fl oz freshly squeezed orange juice

$^1/_2$ fl oz freshly squeezed lemon juice

Dry ginger ale to top up

Method
Shake the cranberry, orange, and lemon juice with ice and strain into a chilled Martini glass. Top up with ginger ale and garnish with a lemon twist.

Cinderellatini

1 $^1/_2$ fl oz freshly squeezed orange juice

1 $^1/_2$ fl oz freshly
pressed pineapple juice

$^1/_2$ fl oz freshly squeezed lemon juice

$^1/_2$ fl oz sugar syrup

1 dash of grenadine

Method
Shake all ingredients with ice and strain into a chilled Martini glass. Garnish with an orange twist.

The earliest known version of the Cinderella story originates from China around 860CE. The heroine, Yeh-Shen, had the smallest feet in the land, an important aspect of beauty in the Chinese culture where foot-binding is common practice. This explains the significance of her foot fitting into a glass slipper. My favorite version of the story is from the brothers Grimm, which has the ugly stepsisters cutting off their toes and heels in order to be able to cram their feet into the crystal footwear. When their deception is exposed they have their eyes pecked out by crows. Nice touch.

martini

glossary

Absinthe—also known as The Green Fairy, this is a highly intoxicating spirit of central European origin. It is extremely high in alcohol, frequently above 70%. It also contains thujone which has a chemical structure very similar to tetrahydrocannibinol (THC), the active compound in cannabis.

Advocaat—a rich and creamy blend of egg yolks, aromatic spirits, sugar, brandy, and vanilla from Holland.

Amaretto—an almond-flavored liqueur made from the apricot kernels. The best-known brand is Disaronno from Saronno in Italy.

Angostura bitters—bitters are a distillation of aromatic herbs, barks, roots, and plants. They are often used as digestive aids and appetite stimulants as well as flavoring agents. Angostura is the most famous brand. Others include Fernet Branca and Peychaud.

Aquavit—or akvavit, is a spirit of Scandinavian origin distilled from grain or potatoes and flavored with caraway seed. It is occasionally flavored with cumin, dill, fennel, or coriander.

Benedictine—a medicinal-tasting herbal liqueur created by Benedictine monks in 1510 in Normandy. The "secret" recipe includes juniper, myrrh, angelica, cloves, cardamom, cinnamon, vanilla, and honey.

Calvados—an apple brandy from Normandy in northern France.

Chambord—a raspberry liqueur.

Chartreuse—a herbal liqueur created by Carthusian monks in the early 1600s. Made from a brandy base, it is flavored with 130 herbs and plants. Green Chartreuse is the only naturally green-colored liqueur and is 55% alcohol. Yellow Chartreuse is sweeter and milder and 40% alcohol.

Clamato—a premixed blend of tomato and clam juice.

Cointreau—a liqueur made from brandy and orange peel. The best-known brand is triple sec, which is 40% alcohol.

Crème de banane—a banana flavored liqueur, usually 30% alcohol.

Crème de caçao—a chocolate-flavored liqueur made from cacao beans and scented with vanilla, usually between 25% and 30% alcohol. It is available in two colors, dark and white (clear).

Crème de cassis—a blackcurrant liqueur, between 18% and 25% alcohol, originating from Dijon, France.

Crème de menthe—peppermint liqueur.

Crème de mure—blackberry liqueur.

Curacao—a sweet, orange-flavored liqueur made with dried peel from

small, green oranges grown in the Dutch West Indies. It is available in blue, orange, and clear varieties, and is often substituted for Cointreau. See "Triple Sec."

Cynar—an Italian liqueur made from artichokes and flavored with quinine.

Drambuie—the leading brand of whisky liqueur, made with heather, honey, and herbs.

Dubonnet—a blend of vermouth, wine, spices, and herbs from the south of France. Dubonnet is available in Blanc and Rouge formats, both at 17% alcohol.

Fernet Branca—an Italian bitters made from herbs with a strong medicinal flavor. See "Angostura bitters."

fraise—strawberry liqueur.

Frangelico—a hazelnut-flavored liqueur from the Piedmont hills in northern Italy. It also contains cacao, coffee, vanilla, and various Italian herbs and spices. 24% alcohol.

Galliano—a yellow liqueur from Italy flavored with star anise and vanilla. 35% alcohol.

Genever gin—a style of gin from Holland, claimed by some to be slightly softer than London dry gin.

Grand Marnier—an orange-flavored, Cognac-based liqueur from the Charente region of France.

Grappa—an Italian spirit distilled from pomace, the leftovers of the winemaking process (grape skins, seeds, and stalks). Nowadays, producers are making single-grape-variety grappas, notably from Chardonnay, Pinot Grigio, and Moscatel.

Grenadine—a sweet, pink syrup made from pomegranates.

Jägermeister—a strongly medicinal-tasting, herbal liqueur from Germany. Supposedly very good for settling the stomach.

Kahlua—a popular brand of coffee liqueur from Mexico. 26% alcohol.

Krupnik—a syrupy, honey-flavored vodka.

Kümmel—a clear liqueur flavored with caraway seed, cumin, and fennel.

Licor 43 (Cuarenta y Tres)—a Spanish liqueur made from 43 fruits and herbs with a vanilla flavor.

Lillet—a French aperitif made from Bordeaux wine and brandy mixed with herbs, fruits, and spices. Available in red or white.

Limoncello—a lemon-flavored liqueur from Italy.

Mandarine Napoleon—a French liqueur made from tangerine skins macerated in grape brandy. 40% alcohol.

Maraschino liqueur—a cherry liqueur made from Maraska cherries grown in Dalmatia in the former Yugoslavia. These are sour-tasting cherries with an almond-like flavor.

Marsala—a fortified wine from around the town of Marsala in western Sicily.

Midori—a popular brand of melon liqueur. 30% alcohol.

Orange bitters—any bitters flavored with orange. See "Angostura bitters."

Orgeat syrup—an almond-flavored syrup.

Parfait Amour—a violet-colored curacao-style liqueur flavored with rose petals, vanilla, and almonds.

Passoa—passion-fruit and citrus liqueur from Spain. 20% alcohol.

Pisang Ambon—an emerald-green, banana-flavored liqueur from Indonesia made from herbs and tropical fruits.

Pisco—a white spirit distilled from grapes, so it's essentially a clear brandy, from Chile and Peru.

Poire William—a sweet, pear-flavored eau de vie, named after a variety of pear the French call Williams Bon-Chretien.

Prosecco—the name of a white grape variety grown near Venice and the sparkling wine made from that variety.

Punt e Mes—a brand of red vermouth blended with bitters.

Sake—Japanese rice wine, usually consumed warm.

Sambuca—a licorice-flavored liqueur from Italy.

Sloe gin—gin infused with sloe berries, the small, sour, blue-black fruit of the blackthorn.

Sweet and sour mix—a pre-mixed blend of sugar syrup, and lemon juice.

Triple Sec—an orange-flavored liqueur, usually sweeter than curacao. See "Cointreau."

Tuaca—an Italian citrus-flavored liqueur with a hint of vanilla.

Zubrowka—vodka flavored with sweet, aromatic bison grass.

martini

index

Absinthe Minded 102
Absolutely Fabulous 30
Acapulco Gold 206
After Eight 122
Alabama Slammer 59
Alamo Splash 82
Alaska 198
Alexander 132
Alexander the Great 104
Allen 164
Allies 31
Almond Joy 120
Alternatini 116
Angel's Delight 113
Anouchka 47
Apple Strudeltini 84
Apricot Mango 88
Aquavit Clamtini 186
Artillery 41
Asian Pear 60
Astoria 32
Atomic Orange 61
Aviation 101
Baby Face 86
Bald Eagle 78
Banoffeetini 106
Barney's Blue Cosmo 57
Basil Beauty 189
Beach Blanket Bingo 204
Bee's Knees 95
Bellinitini 62
Berritini 98
Berry Blue 63
Berry Exciting 71
Berry White 74
Betweenytini 178
Bikinitini 139
Black 64
Black & White 118
Black Beard 110

Black Forest Gateau 115
Black Ice 156
Blackberry 65
Blackthorn English 140
Blood Orange 51
Bloody Bull 181
Blue Monday 79
Blueberry 75
Blues 71
Blue Star 42
Blue Train 66
Blush 107
Bone Dry Diablo 33
Boo Boo's Special 203
Bootleg 119
Bootlegger 141
Boston Bullet 40
Bounty 114
Bourbon Bon Bon 108
Bourbon Milk Punch 129
Brazen 152
Bronx 34
Bronx Terrace 158
Bubbly 191
Buckeye 48
Buff 134
Burnt Almond 109
Busy Bee Sting 142
Butterscotch 129
Cactus Bite 77
Cajun 182
California 200
Cameron 174
Candy Apple 106
Caramel 130
Cardinal Punch 209
Caribou 125
Carlton Cocktail 149
Carpano 143
Carribbean Cocktail 208
Castro 66
CC Bellini 200
Chelsea Sidecar 160
Cherrytini 67

Chihuahua 96
Chill-Out 144
Choco-Coconutini 123
Chocolate 136
Chocolate Biscuit 111
Chocolate Covered
   Strawberrytini 112
Chocolate Lemontini 116
Chocolate Mint 127
Chocolate Orange 113
Chocolate Rum 121
Christmas 137
Cinderellatini 219
Cinnamon Limeade 170
Citron Dragon 87
Claridge 177
Classic Dry Martini 27
Clear-Coin 145
Clover Club 168
Cocoa Peach 114
Cocuba 108
Coffee 115
Collection 173
Colony Club 37
Coolman 68
Copper 162
Coppertone Tan 107
Cosmpolitan, The 50
Cranberry & Mint 79
Crantini 95
Crazy Fin 197
Creole 188
Cuccumber 147
Cupid's Cosmo 54
Dazed and Infused 134
Decadent 112
Desperate 79
Desperate Blackberry 173
Detroit 148
Diablo 199
Diego 148
Diplomat 48
Dirty 35
DNA 147

Doctor's Orders 204
Dorian Gray 69
Double S & M 149
Double Vision 144
Down East Delight 209
Dusty 36
Dutch Breakfast 143
Eager Beaver 133
East Indian 195
Easter 136
Educated Cosmo 54
Egg Custard 117
El Floridita 174
El Niño 60
Elderflower 150
Emerald 151
English 152
Envy 70
Espionage 161
Fantasitini 110
Fare Thee Well 38
Farmer's 31
FDR's 37
Fifty-Fifty 34
Fine and Dandy 158
Fino 193
Flirtini 195
Float Like a Butterfly 141
Floof 192
Florida Twist 100
Florida Rum Runner 64
Flying Dutchman 35
French 85
French Bisontini 89
Fresh Fruitini 72
Fruit Salad 102
Fuzzy 73
Gelardi 153
Get Lucky 218
Gibson 38
Gilroy 42
Gilroy (garlic) 181
Gimlet 45
Gin and It 47

222

index

Gin and Sin 47
Gin Fix 32
Ginger Rogers 121
Ginger Cosmo 52
Ginger Mick 205
Gingerbread Man-Darine
Gingertini 119
Ginitini 39
Gin Sour 40
Girasole 75
Gloom Raiser 40
Golden Nugget 151
Grand Cosmo 56
Grande Champagne
  Cosmo 54
Granny's 100
Grape Expectations 64
Grappatini 163
Great Mughal 169
Greciantini 207
Green 30
Green Eyes 61
Green Fairy 154
Green Hornet 183
Green Jade 125
Groovy 87
Gumdrop 155
Gypsy 41
Hair Raiser 159
Hasty 177
Hawaiian Cosmo 51
Heston 51
Hip Cat 156
Honey & Marmalade 118
Honeydew 100
Honolulu 76
Hoosier 156
Hot & Dirty 184
Hurricane 124
Hyde & Seek 107
I'll Fake Manhattan 216
Imagination 120
Imperial 157
In & Out 36

In the Sack 194
Incognito 140
Ink 76
International Incident 105
Ivy Club 142
Jacktini 152
Jacques Cousteau 101
Jade 159
James Bond 33
Japanese Pear 194
Japanese Slipper 90
Jasmine 42
Jelly Beanytini 120
Jersey Lily 206
Jet Black 159
Jimmy's Beach Cruiser
  211
Julep 155
Jumping Jack Flash 77
Kamikazi 52
Kangaroo 43
Katinka 169
Kee-Wee 95
Kermit 78
Key Lime 114
Key Lime Pie 91
KGB 144
Knockout 118
Kryptonite 79
Kurrant Affair 92
Latino 121
Lava Lamp 160
Lazarus 122
Le Diamant 188
Lemon 69
Lemon & Spice 184
Lemon Aid 94
Leninade 92
Lethal Weapon 207
Limetini 80
Limey 91
Limey Cosmo 55
Limon Cosmo 56
Liquid Lover 166

London 161
Love 151
Low Tide 185
Luxury 162
Lychee 81
Lychee & Rose Petal 87
Mae West 43
Magic Island 207
Magnolia Blossom 84
Mai Lai 82
Maiden's Prayer 35
Mama's 104
Mandarin 59
Mango Madness 97
Martinez 31
Martini Royale 193
Martini Thyme 163
Mary Pickford 172
Melon 83
Melrose 166
Met Manhattan 164
Metropolitan 55
Mexico City 139
Mick Jagger-meister 178
Midnight Black 122
Midnight Mint 111
Milano 198
Mint 130
Miss 80
Mistletoe 165
Mitch 99
Mock Ceasartini 215
Mock Champagnetini 206
Mock Margarita 210
Mock White Sangriatini
  208
Mocktini 202
Moksha 185
Monday Cosmo 55
Monk's 123
Montego Bay 209
Morning Call 119
Mrs Robinson 169
Mule's Hind Leg 161

Mystique 153
Naked 44
Nancy Boy 72
Naughty By Nature 61
Negroni 146
Nevada 85
New Orleans 124
Nicholas 212
Nightmare 164
Ninitchka 132
Nome 193
Noosa Sunset 202
Northern Lights 93
Nursery Fizz 214
Nutty Berrytini 86
Old Fashioned 167
Onion Ring 181
Opal 168
Orange 90
Orgasm 111
Orgasmatini 106
Oriental 125
Oyster 45
Pac-Man 211
Paisley 39
Pappy Honeysuckle 197
Parisian 60
Park Avenue 165
Parma Violet 133
Parrothead 154
Peach Blossom 98
Peach Melba 66
Peanut & Maple 105
Peanut Butter & Jelly
  126
Pear & Elderflower 88
Pearl Diver 87
Pear Shaped 70
Pearls and Lace 211
Peggy Sue's 175
Pepper 187
Peppermint 112
Perrytini 82
Picca 160

martini

Piccadilly 41
Pichuncho 145
Pina Colada Perfecto 212
Pineapple & Cardamom 89
Pineapple & Ginger 89
Pink Champagne 205
Pink Gin 46
Pink Lady 44
Piscotini 170
Playmate 148
Plum Cosmo 56
PMS 203
Poker Face 71
Polish 171
Pompano 90
Pompanski 68
Pomtini 65
Pontberry 62
Pony's Neck 213
Poohtini 116
Prairie Oyster 213
Princess Margaret 213
Purple Haze 91
Pussyfoot 205
Q 171
Raging Bull 186
Raspberry 62
Raspberry Mochatini 113
Raspberry Saketini 196
Rasta's Revenge 97
Rat Pack 166
Razzle Dazzle 83
Red Angel 192
Red Dog 196
Red Earl 183
Red Snapper 188
Red Neck 172
Remy 146
Renaissance 192
Rendezvous 171
Respect 187

Rhubarb & Custard 128
Rhubarb & Lemongrass 92
Ritz Cocktail, The 197
Road Runner 131
Rocky's Caesar 185
Rolls-Royce 39
Rosie's Special Mocktini 217
Rosy Pippin 214
Ruby 93
Rude Cosmo 53
Rum 173
Russian River 150
Safer Sex on the Beach 214
Saint Moritz 128
Sake-politan 195
Sake-tini 198
Saltecca 182
Saltillo 188
Salty Dog 187
San Francisco 99
San Francisco (mock) 212
Sangria 191
Satsuma 84
Scarlet O'Hara 69
Scotch Bounty 108
Sex & Violets 117
Sex and the City Flirtini 199
Shahad 129
Shirley Temple 208
Shrimptini 182
Shrinking Violet 215
Sidecar 143
Sisco Kid 80
Sling 94
Sloe Gin 146
Smartini 110
Smoked Salmon 189
Smoky 46
Smooth & Creamytini

123
Snowball 130
Snowball Special 215
Sonic Blaster 69
Sourpuss 80
Southern Tea-Knee 174
Sparkly Cosmo 57
Spiced Cranberry 95
Star 175
Star Wars 67
Strawberry 96
Strawberry & Balsamic 184
Summer 83
Sunburnt Kiwi 216
Sun Downer 210
Sunset Cool-tini 219
Surfer's Paradise 217
Swedish Blue 94
Tahititini 97
Tainted Cherrytini 63
Tangerinetini 81
Tango 98
Tarte Tatin 126
Teddy Bear 84
Temperance Mocktail 210
Tequila Fanny Banger 99
Thanksgiving 47
Thriller 93
Tiramisu 131
Tomato Cooltini 218
Tootsie Roll 135
Top Banana 100
Topper 124
Transfusion 219
Trifle 104
Turf 39
Turkish Delight 132
Tuxedo 176
Twinkle 199
Ultimate Cranberry 71
Unfuzzy Naveltini 217

Urban Oasis 75
US 192
Vanilla Sensation 116
Vanilla Twist 133
Vanitini 194
Vante 196
Velvet 126
Veneto 176
Venus 145
Veritas 167
Vesuvio 101
Vodka Espresso 134
Waldorf 179
Walnut 109
Watermelon & Basil 77
Watermelon Cosmo 53
Wet 48
Whip 134
Whiskey 159
White Cosmo 57
White Hound 33
White Lady 37
White Satin 135
White Stinger 109
Wibble 59
Witch's Kiss 204
Wonder 200
Wow 178
Xanthia 139
Xena 135
Yahoo! 127
Yankee Prince 136
Zabaglione 127
Zakuski 102
Zero 73
Zeus 105
Zingy Ginger 137